W9-AGJ-310

STOP!

This is the back of the book. You wouldn't want to spoil a great ending!

This book is printed "manga-style," in the authentic Japanese right-to-left format. Since none of the artwork has been flipped or altered, readers get to experience the story just as the creator intended. You've been asking for it, so TOKYOPOP® delivered: authentic, hot-off-the-press, and far more fun!

DIRECTIONS

If this is your first time reading manga-style, here's a quick guide to help you understand how it works.

It's easy... just start in the top right panel and follow the numbers. Have fun, and look for more 100% authentic manga from TOKYOPOP®!

品質第一公式商品
100%
AUTHENTIC
MANGA

TOKYOPOP

Action, comedy and everything in between!

ABENOBASHI™

MAGICAL SHOPPING ARCADE

OT
OLDER TEEN
AGE 16+

©2002 GAINAX and Abenobashi Production Committee
©2002 Ryusei Deguchi
©2004 TOKYOPOP Inc. All Rights Reserved.

www.TOKYOPOP.com

LOVE (TRIANGLES)
CAN DRIVE A GIRL TO THE EDGE.
TOKYOPOP®
Crazy Love Story™
T
TEEN
AGE 13+
©2004 Lee Vin, DAIWON C.I. INC. ©2004 TOKYOPOP Inc. All Rights Reserved.
www.TOKYOPOP.com

TOKYOPOP®

LEGAL DRUG™

When no ordinary prescription will do...

FROM CLAMP
CREATORS OF
CHOBITS
& TOKYO
BABYLON

©2001 by CLAMP. ©2004 TOKYOPOP Inc. All Rights Reserved.

www.TOKYOPOP.com

最遊記

SAIYUKI

5

KAZUYA MINEKURA

SAIYUKI Vol. 5

Created by Kazuya Minekura

Translation - Alethea Nibley & Athena Nibley
Associate Editor - Lianne Sentar
Retouch and Lettering - Eva Han
Production Artist - James Dashiell
Cover Layout - Anna Kernbaum

Editor - Jake Forbes
Digital Imaging Manager - Chris Buford
Pre-Press Manager - Antonio DePietro
Production Managers - Jennifer Miller and Mutsumi Miyazaki
Art Director - Matt Alford
Managing Editor - Jill Freshney
VP of Production - Ron Klamert
President and C.O.O. - John Parker
Publisher and C.E.O. - Stuart Levy

A TOKYOPOP® Manga

TOKYOPOP Inc.
5900 Wilshire Blvd. Suite 2000
Los Angeles, CA 90036

E-mail: info@TOKYOPOP.com
Come visit us online at www.TOKYOPOP.com

SAIYUKI Volume 4 © 2003 KAZUYA MINEKURA
All rights reserved.
Fiirst Published in 2003 by ISSAISHA, Tokyo.
English translation rights arranged with
ISSAISHA through Tuttle-Mori Agency, Inc., Tokyo.
English text copyright © 2004 TOKYOPOP Inc.

All rights reserved. No portion of this book may be reproduced or transmitted in any form or by any means without written permission from the copyright holders. This manga is a work of fiction. Any resemblance to actual events or locales or persons, living or dead, is entirely coincidental.

ISBN: 1-59182-655-1

First TOKYOPOP printing: November 2004

10 9 8 7 6 5 4 3 2 1

Printed in the USA

The Story So Far

After the combination of youkai magic and science caused the youkai-maddening Minus Wave, the beautiful Shangri-La lies in chaos. Three unusual youkai and a Sanzo Priest travel West to stop the revival of Gyumaoh and save their crumbling world...but crumbling among them, too, is the razor-thin patience that barely keeps our heroes from beating each other senseless.

Unable to escape the memory of his late sister and lover, Hakkai suffered at the hands of Chin Yisou and his vengeful psychological torture. As the goal was to break rather than kill Hakkai, Gojyo and the others were one by one targeted by Chin Yisou's sick games. Hakkai ended near the breaking point, but discovering Chin Yisou's ties to his sister's rapist forced Hakkai to make a choice--was he the Cho Gonou of the past, or the Cho Hakkai of the present? Only in releasing his blood-soaked past could he overcome the villain that hailed from it.

Meanwhile, Gyokumen Koushu stepped up her plans to revive Gyumaoh. She removed Kougaiji from Sanzo-hunting duty and instead handed him a new mission: find the other Tenchi Kaigen sutras and donate them to the experimentation...Yisou's true intention...?

Genjyo Sanzo –

A very brutal, worldly priest. He drinks, smokes, gambles and even carries a gun. He's looking for the sacred scripture of his late master, Sanzo Houshi. He's egotistical, haughty and has zero sense of humor, but this handsome 23-year-old hero also has calm judgment and charisma. His favorite phrases are "Die" and "I'll kill you." His main weapons are the Maten Sutra, a handgun, and a paper fan for idiots. He's 177cm tall (approx. 5'10"), and is often noted for his drooping purple eyes.

Son Goku –

The brave, cheerful Monkey King of legend; an unholy child born from the rocks where the aura of the Earth was gathered. His brain is full of thoughts of food and games. To pay for crimes he committed when he was young, he was imprisoned in the rocks for five hundred years without aging. Because of his optimistic personality, he's become the mascot character of the group; this 18-year-old of superior health is made fun of by Gojyo, yelled at by Sanzo and watched over by Hakkai. He's 162cm tall (approx. 5'4"). His main weapon is the Nyoi-Bo, a magical cudgel that can extend into a sansekkon staff.

Sha Gojyo –

Gojyo is a lecherous kappa (water youkai). His behavior might seem vulgar and rough at first glance (and it is), but to his friends he's like a dependable older brother. He and Goku are sparring partners, he and Hakkai are best friends, and he and Sanzo are bad friends (ha ha!). Sometimes his love for the ladies gets him into trouble. Because of his unusual heritage, he doesn't need a limiter to blend in with the humans. His favorite way of fighting is to use a shakujou, a staff with a crescent-shaped blade connected by a chain; it's quite messy. He's 184cm tall (approx. 6'), has scarlet hair and eyes, and is a 22-year-old chain smoker.

Cho Hakkai –

A pleasant, rather absent-minded young man with a kind smile that suits him nicely. It's sometimes hard to tell whether he's serious or laughing to himself at his friends' expense. His darker side comes through from time to time in the form of a sharp, penetrating gaze, a symbol of a dark past. As he's Hakuryu's (the white dragon) owner, he gets to drive the Jeep. Because he uses kikou jutsu (Chi manipulation) in battle, his "weapon" is his smile (ha ha!). He's 22 years old, 181cm tall (approx. 5'11") and his eyes are deep green (his right eye is nearly blind). The cuffs he wears on his left ear are Youkai power limiters.

THREE YEARS EARLIER.

Half the population of a Village was killed two months ago.
And the other day, another thousand of Hyakugan Maoh's tribe.

A THOUSAND YOUKAI, HM?

MASS MURDER...?
That's right.
ゴボッ

Genyo Sanzo.
YES?
We would like you...
...to apprehend this felon.

His name is Cho Gonou.
He's a young man who once was human.

第24話

CHAPTER 24: BE THERE <1>

DAMN, GOJYO. CUT ME SOME SLACK.
OH, WOOOW!
HE DID IT AGAIN!

THE NIGHT'S STILL YOUNG, BOYO.
RELAX. I'M NOT GONNA TAKE EVERYTHING *THIS* EARLY.

TEE HEE HEE!
THEN BE SURE TO WIN, GOJYO. ♡
LISTEN UP, LADIES. I WIN THE NEXT ONE, AND TONIGHT'S ON ME.
ALL RIGHTEE THEN!

...MMM, AND WHAT GORGEOUS HAIR. HOW DID YOU SAY YOU DYE IT?
AND YOUR EYES ARE WINE RED UP CLOSE.
.....
ARE ALL THE CHICKS ON GOJYO'S SIDE? UNBELIEVABLE.
OF COURSE WE ARE.
PUT IT ON MY TAB, BAR-KEEP.
HUH?
THA
RIGHT. THAT'LL DO FOR TODAY.
BEATS ME.
SLAM
REALLY? WHY?
WAY TO GO, IDIOT. GOJYO HATES TALKING ABOUT HIS HAIR.
'TIL NEXT TIME.
G'NIGHT. ♡
WAIT A SEC. GOJYO!

...WINNING WITH A FEW STALE BETS KEEPS THE MEALS COMING.
I GUESS IT WORKS IF I DON'T LOOK ANYONE IN THE EYE.
GORGEOUS HAIR, SHE SAYS.
RIIIGHT.
AND LANDING CHICKS WITH LAME PICKUP LINES GETS ME THROUGH THE NIGHT.
NOT WHEN IT'S THE COLOR OF...
HM?
DAMN. LIFE IS SO EASY IT MAKES ME WANNA PUKE.

WHAT THE HELL?
WAY TO BLOCK THE PATH.
EWW...
THOSE'RE A LOTTA GUTS.
HEY, MAN.
YOU DEAD DOWN THERE?
HUNH.
GUESS THAT'S A NO.

HE LOOKED AT ME...AND SMILED, I THINK.

.....
THIS ISN'T WHAT I EXPECTED.
HELL IS RATHER ANTI-CLIMACTIC.
WHO'RE YOU CALLING ANTI-CLIMACTIC?
ABOUT TIME YOU WOKE UP.

THE DOCTOR WOULDN'T SHUT UP ABOUT HOW YOU HAD TO SLEEP. AND HE WOULDN'T LET ME SMOKE IN HERE.
NOW LET ME SMOKE. NOW.
OH. UM, OF COURSE.

THAT THIS ISN'T HELL, I MEAN.

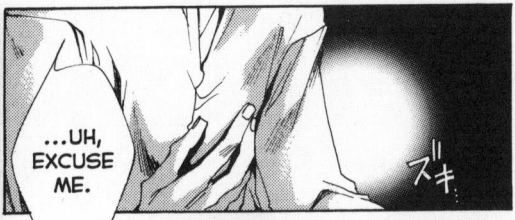
...UH, EXCUSE ME.
ズキ…

*SHARP PAIN

ARE YOU THE ONE WHO HELPED ME?

HUH?
WHY? ARE YOU MAD?

NO.
I'M... GLAD I'M STILL HERE.
THANK YOU VERY MUCH.

I TAKE IT YOU *WANTED* TO DIE.

IS THAT SO? *THANKS.*
I KINDA SHOVED YOUR GUTS BACK IN, BUT YOU SEEM OKAY ENOUGH.
YOU WERE IN A COMA FOR A WEEK. YOU SHOULD BE PRETTY MUCH FIXED UP BY NOW.

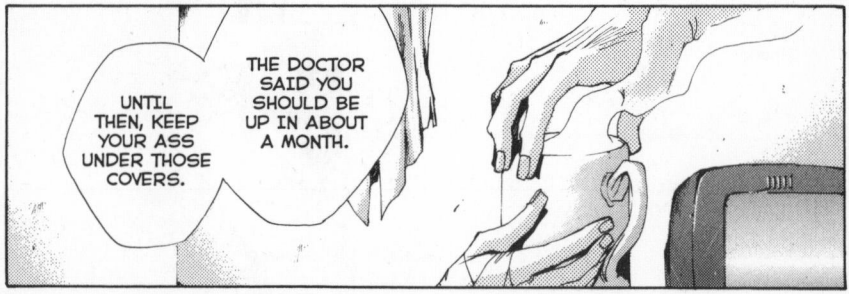
UNTIL THEN, KEEP YOUR ASS UNDER THOSE COVERS.
THE DOCTOR SAID YOU SHOULD BE UP IN ABOUT A MONTH.

THIS IS THE *FIRST* AND *LAST* TIME I BRING A *DUDE* TO MY BED.

.....
YES, SIR.

PRIEST SANZO!
THANK HEAVEN YOU'VE RETURNED!
WHAT IS IT NOW?

AS YOU CAN SEE...

FILTHY
HEY!
SANZO'S HOME. YAAAY! ♡
PANT PANT
DAH!
YOU STUPID MONKEY!
HE BROUGHT THAT MUDDY DOG INTO THE TEMPLE.
IT'S BEEN BREAKING RELICS, AND WE CAN'T SEEM TO CATCH IT.
.....
THAT HURT! WHAT'D YOU DO THAT FOR?
SHUT YOUR MOUTH! WHAT ARE YOU, IN HEAT?
NOW WASH UP AND GET CHANGED.
OW! OW! OW! OW! OW!

THAT BOY IS A PEST.
WHY DID PRIEST SANZO PICK UP SUCH A DEGENERATE IN THE FIRST PLACE?
I HAVE NO IDEA.
AND THE DOG GOES. MOVE!
OKAY ALREADY! WAY TO BE A STINKER!
...FOR THAT, YOU DIE.

WHY DID I BOTHER? IS THAT IT?

EEP!

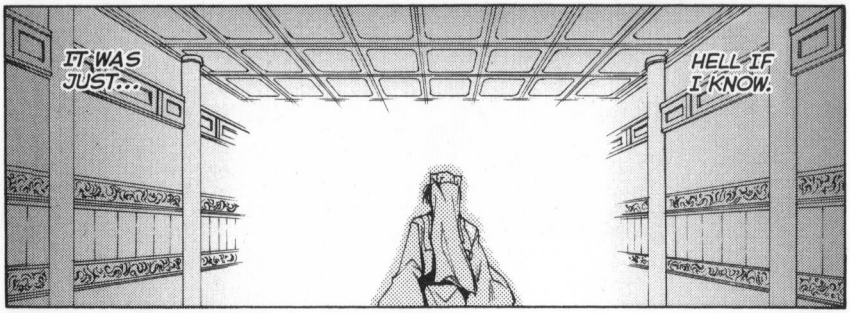
IT WAS JUST...
HELL IF I KNOW.

WHEN I LEFT KINZAN TEMPLE TO RECLAIM MY MASTER'S SUTRA, I DIDN'T EVEN KNOW WHERE TO START.
I'D JUST COME TO THIS TEMPLE. IT WAS THE EASTERNMOST ON THE SHORTEST ROUTE TO INFORMATION.

...HE WOULDN'T SHUT UP.

HIS... INCESSANTLY AGGRAVATING VOICE WOULDN'T STOP CALLING ME.
I FIGURED I'D KNOCK HIM ONE IN THE HEAD.
BUT THEN HE LOOKED UP.
WHEN HE STARED AT ME WITH THAT STUPEFIED LOOK...

...I LOST THE URGE TO HIT HIM.
SHUT THE HELL UP.
C'MON. IT'S NOT LIKE I HAVE A CHOICE.

I JUST GOT AN IRRITATING MISSION TO GO FIND SOMEONE.
I MAY BE GONE AWHILE.
FOR REAL?

SANZO!
BUT REGARDLESS, I KNOW BETTER NOW.
ONE BLOW TO THE HEAD NEVER WOULD'VE CUT IT.

ARE YOU GOIN' SOME-WHERE?
chink
LOOKS LIKE IT.

THEN LEMME COME! ♡
GET SOMEONE ELSE TO TAKE YOU FOR A WALK.
NEVER.

SELF-AWARENESS, MONKEY. LEARN IT.
ARE YOU CALLIN' ME AN ANIMAL?!

...!
SANZO! TAKE ME TAKE ME!
"WHY DID PRIEST SANZO PICK UP SUCH A DEGENERATE IN THE FIRST PLACE?"
BUT IT SUCKS HERE, SANZO!
I DON'T WANNA BE ALONE!
HUH?
ズッ
I CAN'T WIN AGAINST YOUR POWERS OF ANNOYANCE.
JUST CAN IT.
SIT GAWKING LIKE THAT, AND I WILL LEAVE YOU BEHIND.
WHAT'S THE MATTER, GOKU?

FWAP
FULL HOUSE, IT SEEMS.

WAH! WAIT UP, WAIT UP!
SANZO, OI!

AH. SORRY ABOUT THAT.
LIKE HELL I AM.
THOUGH I'M GOING EASY ON ON YOU, SINCE YOU'RE INJURED.
HUNH. YOU'RE NOT BAD AT THIS.

FEH. YOUR BUSINESS AIN'T MINE.

YOU HAVEN'T ASKED ME YET...
...ABOUT MY AFFAIRS.

GOT SOME-WHERE TO GO?
NO.
THOUGH I HAVE JUST ONE THING...
...I NEED TO DO.
I'M SORRY, BUT...
...MAY I STAY HERE UNTIL I'M WELL ENOUGH TO MOVE ON?
IS THAT RIGHT?
OH! A STRAIGHT FLUSH--I'M SORRY.
SORRY.
I JUST HAVE A KNACK FOR THESE THINGS.
YOU SOME KINDA PRO?
GODDAMMIT!
THIS IS HOW I MAKE MY LIVING, Y'KNOW!

THEN JOIN THE CLUB.
JACK OF ALL TRADES AND MASTER OF NONE?
I GUESS THAT'S ME.
BUT READING THE FLOW OF THE GAME CAN ONLY GET ONE SO FAR.
NOTHING COMES WITHOUT A BIT OF *LUCK.*

ザッ
ザッ
HEY, SANZO?

WHO KNOWS?
THIS CHO GONOU KILLED LOTSA GUYS, RIGHT?
HE MUST BE PRETTY BAD.

WHY WOULD THE THREE ASPECTS SEND SOMEONE OF MY STATUS AFTER AN ORDINARY MURDERER IN THE FIRST PLACE?
THIS ENTIRE MISSION IS MAKING ME UNEASY.
WE HAVE NO CLUES BEYOND WHAT THE MAN LOOKS LIKE.

AND HE LEFT EARLY AGAIN YESTER-DAY.
GOJYO'S BEEN REALLY COLD LATELY, DON'T YOU THINK?
...THIS STINKS.
UNLESS THERE'S SOMETHING ELSE GOING ON HERE.
I HEARD HE PICKED UP AN INJURED GUY 'BOUT A MONTH AGO.

MM?
HEY.

CAN YOU TELL ME MORE ABOUT THAT INJURED MAN?

THE DOCTOR SAID IT WAS A DUDE...
...WITH GREEN EYES AND A PRETTY FACE.

WOW. LOOKIT THE BOMB-SHELL WE'VE GOT HERE.
YOU DIG MEN, PRIESTY?
I'LL TELL YOU ABOUT GREEN-EYES.

?!

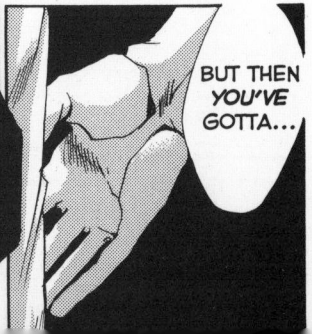
BUT THEN *YOU'VE* GOTTA...

AH, GOJYO-SAN.
I'VE "GOTTA" WHAT?
SHIT-EATING MOTHER-FUCKER.
DO YOU HAVE A MOMENT?
SURE.
BUT BEFORE I GO...
...I'D LIKE TO TELL YOU SOMETHING.
YOU LEAVING ALREADY?
YES.

PERHAPS STAYING HERE SPURRED THE EPIPHANY OF MY SIN.
EPIPHANY?
I'VE KILLED A LOT OF PEOPLE IN THE NAME OF REVENGE.
BUT REALLY, MORE THAN ANYTHING... I DID IT FOR MYSELF.
THANK YOU VERY MUCH FOR HELPING ME.
...AND THEN I'LL ACCEPT WHATEVER PUNISHMENT I DESERVE.
I HAVE ONE LAST ACTION TO TAKE...
IT'S YOUR HAIR AND EYES, GOJYO-SAN.
THEY STRIKE ME AS THE COLOR OF *BLOOD.*

YOUR HAIR AND EYES REMIND ME OF THAT.
THEY'RE LIKE A WARNING, I SUPPOSE.
THE RED THAT STAINED MY HANDS...
...KEPT ME GROUNDED WHEN I TRIED TO ESCAPE THE WEIGHT OF MY CRIMES.

I'LL BE GOING, THEN.
SURE.
.....
'S THAT RIGHT?

MAYBE I WANTED TO MEET HIM.
MAYBE THAT'S IT.

HEY...
...WHO SEES BLOOD IN THE RED I WAS BORN WITH.
I GUESS I'M NOT THE ONLY ONE...

TELL ME SOME-THING.
WHAT'S YOUR NAME?

knock
knock
MY NAME IS--

SORRY TO BOTHER YOU THIS LATE.
I'M LOOKING FOR SOME-ONE.

YEAH, YEAH.
WHO IS IT?

HOLD THAT THOUGHT.

HE'S A YOUNG MAN, AROUND 20, WITH GREEN EYES.
HE'S ALSO A FUGITIVE GUILTY OF MASS MURDER.

HIS NAME IS CHO GONOU.

...WHO?
SORRY. NEVER HEARD OF HIM.

第25話

CHAPTER 25: BE THERE <2>

EAT UNTIL YOU CAN'T ANYMORE.
PLAY UNTIL YOU DROP.
SLEEP THE DAY AWAY.
IT'S OKAY TO LAUGH, OR YELL, OR CRY.
JUST LIVE, LIVE, LIVE.

I'M LOOKING FOR CHO GONOU.
HE'S A MASS MURDERER ON THE RUN.

SORRY, PAL. CAN'T HELP YOU THERE.
DON'T KNOW THE GUY.
VERY FUNNY.
BUT EVERYONE IN TOWN SAID YOU PICKED HIM UP, SO CUT THE BULLSHIT.
I'D SUGGEST YOU STOP HIDING HIM AND GET THE HELL OUT OF HERE.
DO YOU EVEN KNOW WHAT HE DID? HELPING HIM MAKES YOU AN ACCOMPLICE.
……!!

!
I SAID I'VE NEVER HEARD OF HIM.
AND WHY THE HELL'S A PRIEST LOOKING FOR A MURDERER?
.....

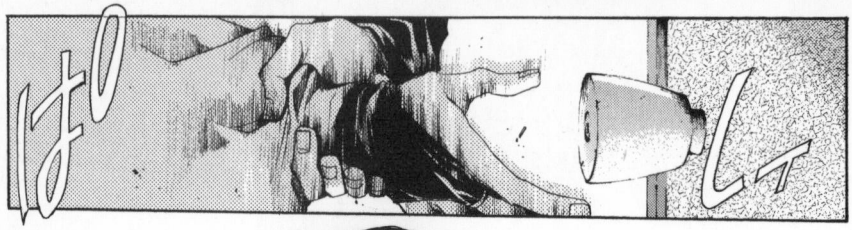

LET GO.
YEAH? AND WHAT IF I DON'T?

!!
HGCK...
GHHK!
HAKGH!
SON OF A...
SHIP
!

...NOW YOU'RE *DEAD,* BASTARD.
HEH.
NOT EXACTLY A *NORMAL* PRIEST, ARE YA?

GOOD LUCK TRYING.
YOU'RE EAGER TO DIE. I CAN HELP YOU OUT WITH THAT.
BOMBSHELL OR NOT, I DON'T ENTERTAIN GUY REQUESTS.
YOUR ATTITUDE'S GOING TO GET YOU KILLED.
NOW MOVE.
THE NEXT ONE WILL IMPROVE THE VENTILATION IN THAT HOT HEAD OF YOURS.
Y-YOU'RE NOT A FRIGGIN' PRIEST!

IS THAT CHO GONOU?
GOJYO-SAN?!
GET YOUR ASS BACK INSIDE!
!
!!

ゴ
NOW HURRY UP AND GO!
I CAN'T HOLD HIM FOR-EVER.
TOO BAD FOR YOU, MY GROUND HOLDS ARE KILLER. ♡
YOU...
...BAS-TARD...

ハッ…
……!
RUN, DAMMIT!
TCH!
GOKU!
ドカーン

YOU BROUGHT A BUDDY?
I'VE JUST GOTTA KNOCK 'IM OUT, RIGHT?
OKAY, SANZO!
……!!
NNGH…
!

DAMN. HE BARELY MANAGED IT...
...BUT HE STILL BLOCKED GOKU.
ー!
THIS GUY MAY BE PRETTY GOOD!
HEEEY, SANZO!
STOP SOUNDING SO HAPPY, MONKEY!
'KAY.
I'LL GET SERIOUS NOW. LOOKIE!
HOP
HAAH...
PING
NNN.
HAA...

ドン
ドン
ドン

HEE HEE.
WHA?!
WHO THE HELL IS THAT KID?!
AT THAT SPEED...
!!

GOKU!
HAH?
NO FAIR!
D-DON'T MOVE. PLEASE.
JUST LISTEN TO WHAT I HAVE TO SAY.
THAT MAN HAS NOTHING TO DO WITH ME.
PLEASE DON'T HOLD HIM RESPON-SIBLE.
I KNOW I'VE COMMITTED VERY SERIOUS CRIMES.
AND I KNOW EVEN MY LIFE ISN'T ENOUGH FOR ATONEMENT.
BUT THERE'S ONE LAST THING...
...I STILL NEED TO DO.

I...I'M SORRY FOR DOING THIS.
PLEASE.
PLEASE JUST GIVE ME A LITTLE MORE TIME.
WHAA?
step
.....
H-HEY!
WAIT A SEC!
DASH

"I HONESTLY WAS..."
#17...
...HOPING TO WAKE UP IN HELL.
I'VE FELT THAT WAY SINCE I LOST SOMEONE DEAR.
YOUR LOVER?
WELL, YES.
THAT'S HALF OF IT.
WHAT'S THAT MEAN?
SHE WAS ALSO MY OLDER SISTER.
...DO YOU THINK LESS OF ME?

WHEN SHE WAS IN DANGER...
...I DIDN'T FEEL A THING.
I WAS PLAYING WITH MY STUDENTS AT THE TIME.
OUTSIDE OF THAT, WE TRIED NOT TO ADVERTISE THE FACT.
WE WERE RAISED IN SEPARATE ORPHAN-AGES.
IT WASN'T EXACTLY TALKED ABOUT.
I GUESS SOME PEOPLE... GO FOR THAT.
AH, WHAT-EVER.
?
PEOPLE OFTEN HAVE A SIXTH SENSE ABOUT LOVED ONES, RIGHT?
BUT STILL.
...REALITY'S A BITCH.
WHY DIDN'T I SENSE SOMETHING AND RUN HOME?
WHY IS THAT, I WONDER?

AH, HELL. LIKE I'M ONE TO TALK.
YOU CAN'T BLAME ALL THAT CRAP ON YOURSELF.
IT WASN'T BECAUSE YOU DIDN'T LOVE HER ENOUGH.
I DON'T HAVE ANYTHING IMPORTANT IN MY LIFE.
I GUESS I WOULDN'T REALLY KNOW.
WHAT EXACTLY IS LOVE?
NOT THAT I WANT IT, PARTICULARLY...
YOU DON'T NEED LOVE TO GET LAID.
JUST ONCE, I THINK I WANNA KNOW.
.....

AS A LESSON TO MYSELF, I GUESS YOU COULD SAY. I THOUGHT I WAS THE ONLY ONE WHO SAW THAT RED AS THE WARNING COLOR OF BLOOD.
I GREW OUT MY HAIR TO COVER THE SCARS FROM WHEN MY MOTHER TRIED TO KILL ME.
...WE'RE WATCHING ILLUSIONS FADE INTO A SEA OF BLOOD.
THE LOVE I COULDN'T GET, AND THE LOVE HE COULDN'T PROTECT.
WHILE BLAMING OUR OWN POWERLESSNESS...
YOU REALLY DIDN'T ASK HIM ANYTHING?
THAT'S WHAT I'VE BEEN SAYING ALL ALONG.
ANY-WAY...
SO. CHO GONOU, HUH?
THE NAME DOESN'T FIT HIM.
ゴクン

HEEEY! THIS IS YUMMY!
CAN I EAT IT ALL?
WHY DO I HAVE TO FEED YOUR DAMN PET?!
APPARENTLY GOKU HASN'T EATEN IN 500 YEARS.
HIS BODY'S MAKING UP FOR LOST TIME.
WHAT'D YOU SAY?
I HOPE YOU'RE KIDDING.
YOU PLANNIN' TO CLEAN ME OUT, MONKEY?
DROP THE GOODS!
I'M NOT A MONKEY, I'M SON GOKU! NYAA!
GIMME GIMME!
SHUT IT! STUPID MONKEY FITS YOU BETTER.
BUT YOU STILL MAKE ME WONDER.
WHY HIDE GONOU AND GET IN TROUBLE FOR IT?
WHY?
BEATS THE HELL OUTTA ME.

I DUNNO, IT'S WEIRD.
HE DIDN'T SEEM REAL BAD TO ME.

HEY, SANZO.
IS GONOU A BAD GUY?
WHAT WAS THAT?

THERE ARE TIMES WHEN IT'S KILL OR BE KILLED. AND THE WORLD'S ROTTING WITH ALL THE PEOPLE WHO *DESERVE* TO DIE.
KILLING ISN'T LIMITED TO EVIL PEOPLE.

BUT LISTEN, GOKU.
PEOPLE WHO LIVE BY KILLING CAN'T EXPECT TO BE SPARED.
KARMA SEES TO THAT.

WHETHER THIS WORLD IS EVIL OR NOT...
...THE ONES WITH THE STRONGEST WILL TO LIVE ARE THE ONES WHO SURVIVE.
HUNH...
THE WILL TO LIVE.
HA HA
WHAT A SHAME YOU BECAME A MONK.
WHAT'S THAT SUPPOSED TO MEAN?
HANDS OFF.

BAH. I THINK YOU'RE WASTING YOUR TIME.
WE'LL HAVE TO GO AFTER HIM.
NO. THIS IS A MISSION, AS MUCH AS IT PAINS ME TO SAY SO.
YEAH?
BUT HE GOT AWAY, SANZO. IZZAT OKAY?

BUT ONCE HE'S DONE IT...
I DON'T KNOW WHAT HE HAD TO DO.

HE SEEMS THE TYPE.
...HE'LL PROBABLY DIE.

LET'S GO, GOKU.
SORRY FOR THE TROUBLE.
HANG ON A SEC.
WHICH IS ALL THE MORE REASON TO GO AFTER HIM.
I'VE BEEN ORDERED TO BRING CHO GONOU TO SHAYOU PALACE.
THIS MISSION IS BAD ENOUGH WITHOUT HIM DYING ON ME.

IF LETTING HIM DIE IS THE KIND THING TO DO...
...THEN I...
I WANNA GO TOO.

...MUST BE ONE SELFISH BASTARD.
Huff
Huff
OW.
HAH
HAH
I MUST HAVE REOPENED THAT WOUND.
I'M NOT SURPRISED.
I WONDER IF GOJYO-SAN'S ALL RIGHT.
I WAS A BURDEN ON HIM UNTIL THE VERY END.
AND I ACCIDENTALLY TOOK THAT GUN.
I DOUBT I'LL BE ABLE TO GIVE IT BACK NOW.

ニャラ…

WITH YOUR REMAINS, I AT LEAST WANT TO...
...WITH THESE TWO HANDS, I STILL WANT TO...

KANAN.
NOT MUCH LONGER NOW.

……

ゴ!!

……?!!
HOUK..
THERE YOU ARE, CHO GONOU.
IT'S ABOUT DAMN TIME.
GGG..
DO YOU REMEMBER THE FACES OF MY FAMILY?

...HUH?
TELL ME YOU REMEMBER SOMETHING OF YOUR VICTIMS, MURDERER!
OR THE FACES OF ALL THOSE VILLAGERS?

第26話

CHAPTER 26: BE THERE <3>

I CAN'T BELIEVE I FINALLY FOUND YOU.
HERE.
I WANTED TO GIVE YOU THIS.
.....!!
TOSS

SOME-THING WRONG?

I CAN GUESS WHERE HE'S HEADED.
PROBABLY TOWARD...
...HYAKUGAN MAOH'S CASTLE--

UH, NO.
I'M JUST... HEARING THINGS. I THINK.

HEY, PRIEST.
WHAT'S GONNA HAPPEN TO HIM IF YOU CATCH HIM?

YOU'RE IN DANGER OF SOUNDING ATTACHED.
AFTER I SAVED HIS DAMN LIFE?
A STUPID DEATH WOULD PISS ME OFF.
I DON'T KNOW HIS PUNISH-MENT.
IT'S UP TO THE THREE ASPECTS, REALLY.
OI.
PAT
YOU'RE A PRETTY HIGH PRIEST, YEAH? THEN YOU PROBABLY KNOW.
WHAT DO RED HAIR AND EYES MEAN?

SO DO I.
CALL ME GREEDY IF YOU HAVE TO...
AN UNBREAKABLE CURSE.
...BUT I WANT THE GUY TO LIVE.
.....
THE COLOR OF BLOOD.
HE THINKS THIS RED IS FOR PENANCE.
YOU'RE AS STUPID AS YOU LOOK.
WHA?
EXACTLY WHAT ARE YOU EXPECT-ING?

*SHAVING THE HEAD IS ASSOCIATED WITH BECOMING A BUDDHIST MONK.

HUH?
BLAH. IT'S AS COLD AS THE REST OF YA.
WHAT IS IT WITH YOU TWO MAKING ME BALD?!
WHAT THE HELL WAS THAT, CHIMPY?!
I THOUGHT IT MIGHT BE HOT.
IT'S AS BRIGHT AS SOMETHIN' BURNIN'.
YOU'RE AS STUPID AS YOU LOOK.

I TRIED TO SAVE SOMEONE WHO THOUGHT I WAS IMPORTANT.
I-I GREW MY HAIR OUT.
EXACTLY WHAT ARE YOU EXPECT-ING?
...IS ME.
BUT THE ONE WHO WANTS TO BE SAVED...

ピク...

?!
WHICH WAY?

WHAT IS IT?
I'M SMELLIN' BLOOD.

RIGHT. MOVE!
UM... OVER THERE!
HERE THEY ARE.
FROM WHEN YOU TOOK MY BROTHER ...
...AND RIPPED HIS EYES OUT.

THE SACRIFICE OF YOUR SINGLE LOVER SAVED ALL THOSE HUMANS.
BUT YOU...
... DESTROYED EVERYTHING THAT SACRIFICE WAS FOR!
IT'S MY TURN, BASTARD.
YOU'RE GONNA PAY FOR MY FAMILY AND EVERYONE ELSE!
WE TOOK AWAY EACH OTHER'S FAMILIES.
WE'RE ALMOST EVEN.
WILL GIVING YOU MY EYES BE ENOUGH?
...IS THAT IT?

?!!
BE MY GUEST.
IT'S NOT AS IF I NEED THEM.
HEY!

ALL RIGHT.
LET ME GET YOU THE OTHER ONE.

I UNDERSTAND HOW YOU FEEL.
S-SON OF A...
CUT...

...THAT ...
...OUT! ARGH!
WHAT THE-- OW!
OW OW OW!
WHAT'RE YOU DOIN', STUPID?!
HUH?
THAT'S NOT COOL!
I THINK YOUR EYES ARE REALLY PRETTY!
GRUNGH

REPENTANCE TO WHOM?
THE GODS?
THE GODS DON'T SAVE ANYONE.
YOU HAVE TO SAVE YOURSELF.
YOU CAN CHOOSE TO DIE.
YOU CAN CHOOSE TO RUN...
WAS IT YOU WHO SAID RED IMPLIES REPENTANCE?

IF YOU REALLY WANT THINGS TO CHANGE...

...YOU'RE GOING TO HAVE TO LIVE.

...BUT DYING ALONE WON'T CHANGE A THING.
TRUST ME ON THAT ONE.

WHO'RE YOU?
ARE YOU DEFENDING THIS GUY?!
NOT QUITE.
JUST REMEMBER...
PEOPLE WHO KILL CAN'T EXPECT TO BE SPARED.
KARMA SEES TO THAT.
WE KNOW YOU WANNA KILL HIM.
GO AHEAD-- WE WON'T STOP YOU.

OR SO SAYS SOME WORLDLY MONK.
WHATEVER THAT'S WORTH.

NNGH!
J-JUST DIE, YOU SICKO!

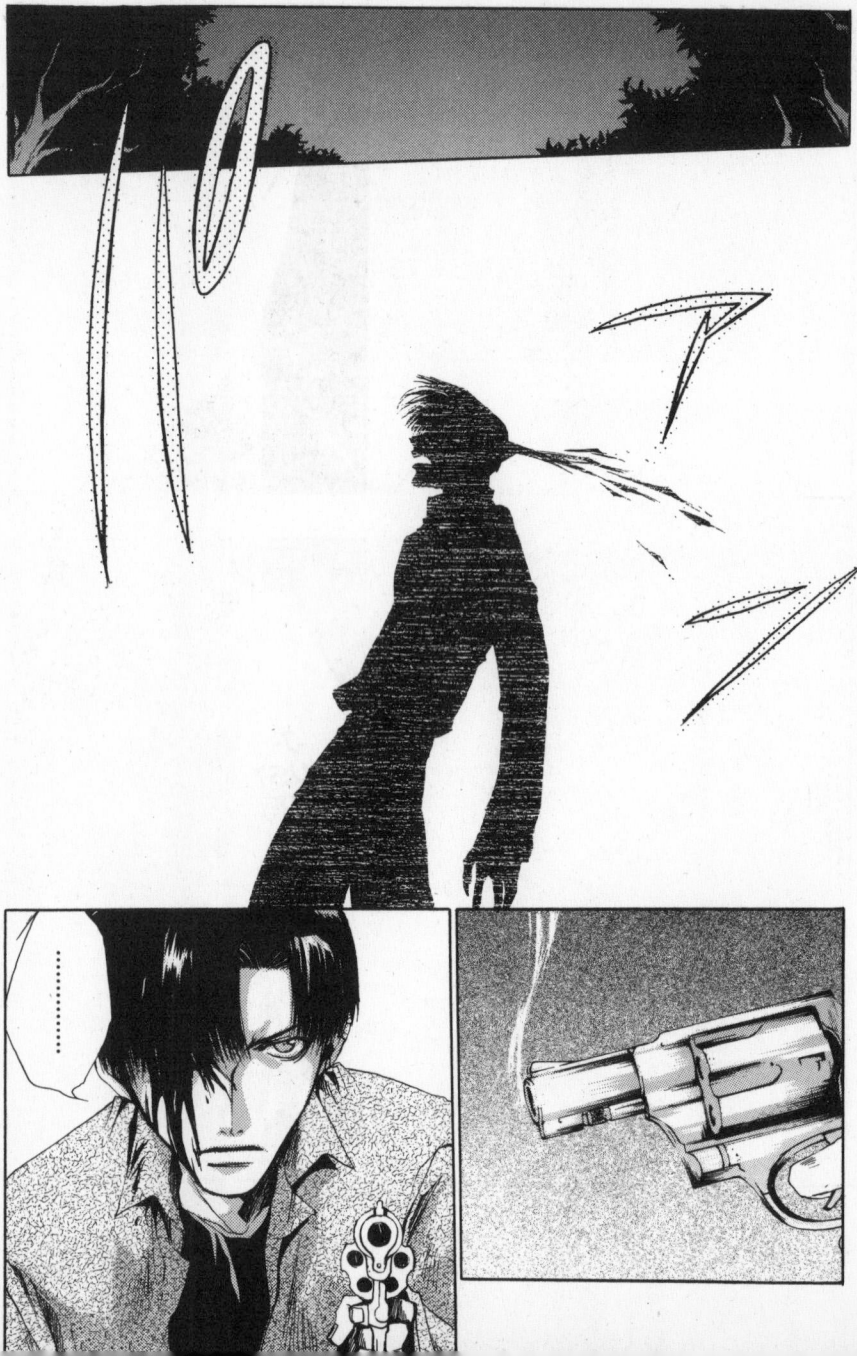

IT DOESN'T MATTER WHERE I LOOK.
IT'S ALWAYS *IDIOTS* AS FAR AS THE EYE CAN SEE.

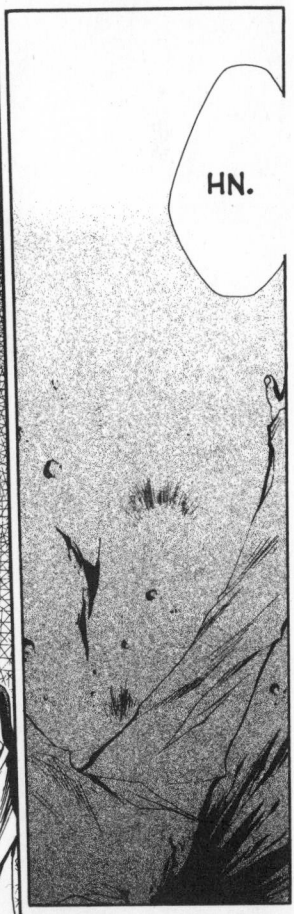
HN.

CHO GONOU.

CAN YOU WALK?
UM, YES.

I HOPE YOU LIKE COMPANY.
HUH?

WE'RE ALL GOING TO HYAKUGAN MAOH'S.

.....
I'D APPRECIATE THAT.

WHAT... HAPPENED...?
A FIRE, IT LOOKS LIKE.
SOMEONE PROBABLY BURNED THE CASTLE DOWN A FEW DAYS AGO.

NOT MUCH LEFT, IS THERE?
...SO THAT'S IT, THEN.

AGAIN.
I COULDN'T SAVE HER *AGAIN.*
DUDE. READ A *SUTRA* OR SOME-THING.
C'MON, MR. WORLDLY PRIEST.
HUNH.
I DON'T THINK IT WOULD HELP MUCH.

.....
crunch
C'MON, MAN.
IS THAT A REASON NOT TO?
FINE. BUT WHEN I READ A SUTRA ...
...IT'S NOT FOR THE DEAD.
ぱっ

IT'S LIKE ALL THE CONFLICT IN US HAS VANISHED.

TODAY, ALL OF US...
I DIDN'T KNOW HIS VOICE COULD GET SO CLEAR.

オ
オ
オ
...HAVE BEEN BROUGHT TOGETHER UNDER THIS GOLDEN LIGHT.

THERE'S NO NEED FOR THAT.

PLEASE CONTINUE.

BUT...
I DON'T MIND, REALLY.

.....

CLANK

Priest Genjyo Sanzo, criminal Cho Gonou.
Enter and come forth.

"IT'S AS BRIGHT AS SOMETHIN' BURNIN'. I THOUGHT IT MIGHT BE HOT."

"BUT DO YOU SERIOUSLY THINK BLOOD IS THE ONLY THING THAT'S RED IN THIS WORLD?"

"THEY'RE LIKE A WARNING, I SUPPOSE."

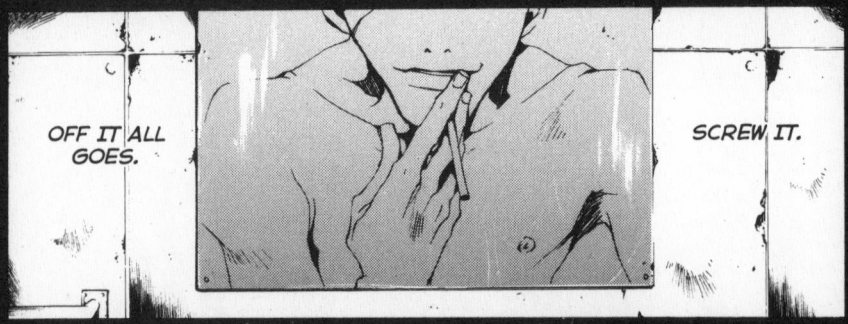

I'M THE ONE WHO WANTS TO BE SAVED.

第27話
CHAPTER 27:
BE THERE
<4>

"CHO GONOU IS DEAD."

NO ONE CAN INTERFERE WITH THE FATE HE CHOSE.
NOT YOU, AND NOT ME.
CLOP.
SON OF A... BITCH.
THIS IS THE SECOND TIME A HOTTIE'S DUMPED ME.
WERE YOU FLATTERING YOURSELF?
.....
I GUESS I WAS.

GOJYO ?!
OMIGOD, IT REALLY IS YOU!
YO. LONG TIME.
WHAT HAPPENED TO YOUR HAIR?!
OH.
JUST... STUFF.
WE HAVEN'T SEEN YOU PLAY CARDS IN FOREVER, MEANIE.
NAH, I STILL PLAY.
I CAN'T EAT IF I DON'T WIN SOME HANDS.

THOUGH I DID GET CLOSE TO THIS GORGEOUS BLOND WHO WAS A REAL BITCH...
...AND THIS OTHER TART WHO'S A BIT LACKING IN THE BRAINS DEPART-MENT.
AND THAT'S NOT COUNTING THE TRAGIC AND EMOTIONALLY SCREWED BEAUTY.

THAT OLD ROUTINE!
IS THERE SOME OTHER WOMAN, GOJYO?!

I WISH.

HUH?
WHAT ARE YOU SAYING?
SEE YA LATER.
HEY, WAIT! GOJYO!
OOOOH!

IT'S NOT LIKE ANYTHING'S CHANGED.
RIGHT.

MISS? ONE OF THESE.
YES, SIR.
BUT...I'M STARTING TO THINK THAT'S OKAY.

WHEN MY HAIR GROWS BACK, IT'LL STILL BE RED.
AND MY RED EYES'LL ALWAYS STARE BACK FROM THE MIRROR.

THESE ARE SUCH A BEAUTIFUL RED, AREN'T THEY?

GOJYO.

HEY, MISSY.
ON SECOND THOUGHT, I'LL TAKE *FOUR.*
...GUESS YOU COULD SAY THAT.

WOOOOW! YOU GUYS!
I HAVEN'T SEEN YA IN FOREVER!

SHUT IT, MONKEY.
SORRY FOR THE INTRU-SION.
GAH!
GOJYO'S HAIR'S ALL STUPID! HA HA!
OI.
YOU TRICKED ME, YOU CHEATING PRIEST!
WHAT ARE YOU TALKING ABOUT?

COOL!
YOU'RE FREE NOW, YAH?
I AM.
I'M GONNA DANCE ON YOUR FREAKIN' GRAVE.
CRIMINAL OR NO, WE CAN'T EXECUTE ANYONE.
BUDDHISM FORBIDS KILLING.
YOU HAVE A BRAIN. USE IT.

HE PLED MY CASE BEFORE THE THREE ASPECTS.
SANZO WAS KIND ENOUGH TO SPEAK ON MY BEHALF.

YEAH? SO WHAT'S YOUR NAME NOW?
...AND BEGUN A NEW LIFE.
I'VE GIVEN UP THE NAME CHO GONOU...

HAKKAI.
YOU LIKE IT?
...HAK-KAI.
MM! IT'S BETTER'N YOUR LAST NAME.
YOU THINK SO?
HOW'S THE ARTIFICIAL EYE DOING?
HAKKAI HAKKAI HAKKAI HAKKAI HAKKAI HAKKAI!
DON'T MAKE FUN OF ME! I CAN REMEMBER!
LET'S SEE HOW LONG YOUR ITTY BITTY BRAIN CAN REMEMBER THAT.
VERY WELL, THANK YOU.

HE NEEDS HELP REMEMBERING GARBAGE DAY.
IT'S A REASON FOR CONCERN.
I'M STARTING TO THINK HE'S SUB-MONKEY.
AND I, AH...
...
CONVINCED GOJYO TO LET ME STAY WITH HIM.
HEY!
GYAH!
YOU KNOW?
IT'S ODD, THOUGH. I'VE SEEN DEATH SO MANY TIMES.
BUT NOW...
...I'M HONESTLY AFRAID TO DIE.

NAH, HAKKAI!
HUH?
I WON'T FORGET YOUR NEW NAME!
SO DON'T CHANGE IT ANYMORE, 'KAY?
.....
WE HAVE A DEAL.

ANY STRUGGLING'S JUST A BIG FAT WASTE OF TIME.
YOU.
IS THAT NEW MOP OF YOURS SUPPOSED TO CHANGE SOMETHING?
NAH.
IT'S A LOT LIKE HAKKAI'S DEAL.
WELCOME TO LIFE.
EVERYTHING'S A USELESS STRUGGLE UNTIL YOU DIE.

BETTER THAN YOUR PATHETIC ANGST.
WELL? DO YOU LIKE THE CUT?
WHAT IS IT NOW?
.....

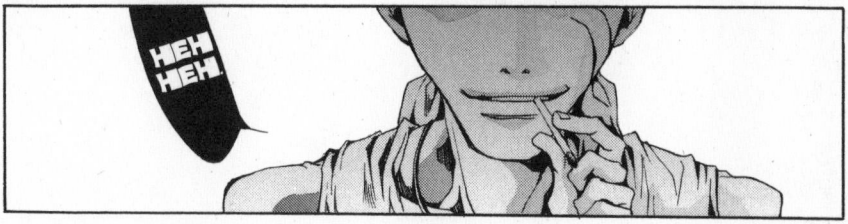
HEH HEH

HGG
HGG
HGG
ARE YOU LOOKING FOR A FIGHT?
THEN GROW IT BACK OUT IT IS.
♪
I'M A PERV, SO IT GROWS FAST.

ALL RIGHTEE!
I'M STARVING, SO LET'S GO LAND SOME FOOD.
WHEEE!
ALL RIGHT!
YIPEE! YIPEE!
JUST KEEP IT DOWN.
C'MON, SANZO! CHOW TIME!
WHAT, ME?
HMPH...
ONLY IF YOU'RE BUYING.

PRIEST SANZO, WHERE ARE YOU GOING?
THERE'S STILL BUSINESS YOU HAVEN'T--
SHUT UP AND GO TO HELL.
B-BUT PRIEST SANZO!

WOW.
WHAT A BEAUTIFUL DAY.

EXCUUUSE ME!
TEACHER! ARE BANANAS A GOOD SNACK ?
SILENCE. NOW.
THEN NEXT TIME WE SHOULD PACK LUNCHES, YES?
DAMN STRAIGHT. PICNIC WEATHER.
YOU'RE ANNOYING ME ALREADY.
DEATH IS SEEMING MORE AND MORE PREFERABLE TO YOU LOT.

CLACK
KANZEON BOSATSU.
WHAT? NO TAKE-BACKS?
ABOUT SANZO AND HIS COMPANY.

JUST NOW...
...I THINK I REALIZED WHY YOU CHOSE THOSE FOUR.

YOU'RE DIGGING WAY TOO DEEP.
IT'S NOTHING THAT FANCY.
I DO STAND BY THAT NOTION.
BUT BEINGS LIKE THAT... THEY'RE SOME-TIMES MORE ELOQUENT THAN ANY DOCTRINE.
THEY CERTAINLY IMPLY THEY'D BREAK ALL COMMANDMENTS WITHOUT A SECOND THOUGHT.

THOSE GUYS JUST HAPPENED TO BE THERE.
第28話
CHAPTER 28:
SANDSTORM

TOO...
...HOT.

AN' WHAT'S WITH TH' BLANKETS IN THIS SUN? BLAH!
DITCH IT IF YOU WANT TO BE COERED IN SAND, MONKEY.
GODDAMMIT! YOU MADE ME GET SAND IN MY MOUTH!
SCOOT OVER. IT'S TOO HOT FOR YOUR CRAMPIN'!
THERE'S NO ROOM TO SCOOT, YOU FRIED MONKEY!
WHA?! THEN YOU'RE A... DRIED-OUT KAPPA!
THE GRAVE IS PLEASANTLY COOL.
AH HA HA!
I'M AFRAID THEY WOULD ROT BEFORE THEY COULD ENJOY IT.
W-WE'LL SHUT UP.
DAMN.

HAKKAI, IS THIS DESERT REALLY A SHORTCUT?
THE MAP SAYS IT ISN'T AS BIG AS IT SEEMS.
THOUGH IT DOES INTERFERE WITH ONE'S SENSE OF DIRECTION.
SAND, SAND, SAND. BAH.
JUST LOOKING AT THE HEAT WAVES IS MAKING ME HOTTER.
WOULD YOU LIKE A SCARY STORY TO COOL YOU OFF? ♪
I KNOW PLENTY.
UH, NO.
THE LAST PERSON I WANT FREAKING ME OUT IS YOU, HAKKAI.
HUH?
CHECK IT OUT.

HEY! GUY IN TH' BLANKETS!
DO YA LIVE NEAR HERE?
AND DO YOU KNOW HOW MUCH FARTHER THIS DESERT EXTENDS, PLEASE?

SURE. YOUR MAP'S A LITTLE OUTDATED. THE DESERT'S BIGGER NOW.
YOU SHOULD BE THROUGH IN ANOTHER NIGHT.
FOR REAL?! ARRGH!
THAT DOES CAUSE SOME PROBLEMS.

YOU'RE TRAVELERS, RIGHT?
MY VILLAGE ISN'T FAR FROM HERE.
COME ON--I'LL SHOW YOU A PLACE TO STAY.

THANK YOU FOR ALL THE HELP, BOTH OF YOU.

TRAVELERS GET LOST IN THESE PARTS A LOT.
LUCKY THIS FELLA BUMPED INTO YOU.

A YEAR AGO, THE DESERT SUDDENLY EXPANDED AND SWALLOWED THE VILLAGE UP.
WE'RE JUST THE ONES WHO CAN'T LEAVE.

PARDON ME FOR ASKING ...
...BUT WHY IS THERE A VILLAGE OUT HERE?
HM. RIGHT.
THIS PLACE *USED* TO BE A DECENT TOWN.

IS THAT RIGHT?
I GUESS THAT'S ANOTHER FORM OF THE SPREADING CHAOS.
HUH?
?
WHO WANTS TO KNOW?
...ARE YOU A SANZO PRIEST?!
THOSE ROBES YOU'RE WEARING!
DON'T TELL ME...
WHATSA MATTER?

I'M SORRY, BUT YOU CAN'T STAY HERE.
FIND SOME OTHER PLACE TO SLEEP!
.....
.....
SLAM!
WHAA?
WHY THE HELL--
WHAT WAS THAT?
HOW SHOULD I KNOW?
DO YOU KNOW SOMETHING OF THIS, LITTLE ONE?
WE'D APPRECIATE YOU SHARING.
.....

...ABOUT A Y-YEAR AGO.
WHEN THIS PLACE WAS STILL PART OF THE TOWN...
...A SANZO PRIEST CAME THROUGH.
HE WAS JUST RESTING FROM A TRIP--LIKE YOU GUYS.
THE WHOLE TOWN HEARD ABOUT IT AND WANTED TO COME SEE.
BUT A YOUKAI FROM THE DESERT HEARD ABOUT HIM TOO.
SHE CAME TO EAT THE SANZO PRIEST.

↑NOT QUITE RIGHT.

SO?
WHAT HAPPENED TO TH' SANZO?
SHIT. IS THAT REALLY TRUE?
HELL IF I KNOW.
HAVING NEVER BEEN EATEN, I WOULDN'T KNOW.
THE MONKS WITH HIM TRIED TO FIGHT THE YOUKAI.
THEY DIDN'T STAND MUCH OF A CHANCE, SO THE SANZO ENDED UP TAKEN.
THOUGH THE YOUKAI LEFT US ALONE AFTER THAT... THE DESERT'S GOTTEN WIDER SINCE THEN.
THE NIMROD LET HIMSELF GET EATEN?
BUT HE WAS A FRICKIN' SANZO.
A SANZO ISN'T NECESSARILY OFFENSIVELY POWERFUL.

OOOOH. SO THAT'S WHY.
I'M SURE HE WAS A PROPER, UPRIGHT, NORMAL SANZO.
ARE YOU IMPLYING SOME-THING?

I'M SORRY. THE PEOPLE HERE ARE NICE, REALLY.
NAH-- YA CAN'T HELP BEIN' SCARED. 'S OKAY!

THAT'D MAKE US BEING HERE A DANGER TO THE VILLAGERS.
MAKES SENSE. I DON'T BLAME 'EM FOR BEING DODGY.

.....
WE SHOULD PROBABLY LEAVE SOON, THEN.

DO YOU KNOW WHERE THAT DESERT YOUKAI'S BASE IS?
UM, I HAVE AN IDEA.

IS SOMETHING WRONG, SANZO?
SORT OF.

HEY, KID.
YES?

YOU WANNA KILL THAT THING?
SINCE WHEN ARE *WE* HEROES?
AN' SHE'S GONNA WANNA EATCHA, SANZO!
THAT THING'S PROBABLY WAY OUT OF THE WAY.

THEN TAKE US THERE.
HEY, WAIT A SECOND!

WAIT.
THAT'S YOUR "ULTERIOR MOTIVE" FACE.
.....
MAYBE.

OUT FOR A WEE STROLL?

GODSPEED, YOUR HIGHNESS.

I DON'T HAVE TIME FOR YOUR SICK HUMOR.
EXCUSE US.
THEY SAY YOU'VE BEEN TAKEN OFF THE SANZO CASE?

IF IT ISN'T NI JIANYI.
GOOD DAY TO YOU. ♡

NOT THIS FREAKSHOW.

AND THIS IS ALL FOR YOUR DEAR MOTHER?
IT'S ENOUGH TO MAKE A GUY CRY.
sob sob
.....
APPARENTLY ONE OF THE TENCHI KAIGEN SUTRAS IS IN THE DESERT TO THE EAST.
BAH.
FORGET HIM, KOU.
GYOKUMEN KOUSHU MADE ME HER SUTRA FETCHBOY A WHILE AGO, NI.
AH, BUT I HAVE SOME-THING I THINK YOU'D LIKE.
SANZO'S NOT MY PROBLEM ANYMORE.

AREN'T YOU CURIOUS ABOUT THE GREATER TRUTH BEHIND ALL THIS?
WOULDN'T YOU LIKE TO KNOW ABOUT THE CORRUPT PARADISE THAT IS SHANGRI-LA?
I HAVE A FEW TASTY TIDBITS FOR YOU.
TAKE THE CHILDREN OF TABOO, FOR INSTANCE.
WHY IS HUMAN-YOUKAI INTERBREEDING FORBIDDEN IN THE FIRST PLACE?
EVERY LEGEND HAS A TIE TO HISTORY.
AND SCIENCE HELPS US PROVE RUMOR, OF COURSE.

CHILDREN BORN BETWEEN DIFFERENT SPECIES...
...CAN'T GENERALLY REPRODUCE, YOU KNOW.
.....!!
THAT'S SOMETHING I LOOKED INTO MYSELF, BUT THERE'S PROOF.
THE CHAOS FROM MIXING YOUJUTSU AND SCIENCE...
...CAN BE ADDRESSED EVEN ON A GENETIC LEVEL.

I WANT THE TRUTH.
IN THE FORM OF SOMETHING I CAN SEE, OF COURSE.
WHO THE HELL ARE YOU?
WHAT ARE YOU REALLY AFTER?
I'M JUST AN ORDINARY SCIENTIST.

OH.
AND ONE MORE THING.

BE SURE TO HOLD ON TO WHAT'S MOST IMPORTANT...
...YOUR HIGH-NESS.
LATER!

OOO...
NIIIIIIII-CHAAAAAN!
.....
BUT THAT'S A SUCKY PLAN!
BE GOOD AND WAIT HERE.
YOUR MOTHER SAID TO KEEP YOU IN THE CASTLE.
YOU TRYIN' TO GO SOMEWHERE WITHOUT LIRIN AGAIN?!
YAONE SPILLED.
FORGIVE ME, LORD.
I'M AFRAID IT SLIPPED OUT.
YAAAAAAAH?
HAVE A GOOD TRIP.
I'LL BRING YOU BACK SOMETHING, UH, YUMMY.
HOW'S THAT?

ONII-CHAN?
SAVE IT FOR SOMEONE WHO DOESN'T ALREADY KNOW.

BE SURE TO HOLD ON TO WHAT'S MOST IMPORTANT.

OF COURSE, MY LORD.

LIRIN'S YOURS, YAONE.
TAKE CARE OF HER.

YOU CAN LOOK, BUT YOU WON'T FIND IT.
AH, TRUTH.

THE PEOPLE I LOVE...
...ARE ALREADY WHAT I LIVE FOR.

ALL THAT EXISTS IS WHAT I CAN TOUCH.
SQUEEZE

UNENDING DESERT WASTELAND.
THE BOY SAID FIVE KILOMETERS NORTH BY NORTHEAST--THAT'S HERE.
IS THIS REALLY TH' PLACE?
IT'S JUST A WHOLE LOTTA NOTHIN'.

HOW TH' HECK'RE WE SUPPOSED TO GET IN?
FOR REAL?
THE YOUKAI CASTLE, I MEAN.
IT'S SUPPOSED TO BE IN THE SAND, RIGHT?

...HIS BELONGINGS SHOULD BE IN THAT CASTLE.
INCLUDING THE TENCHI KAIGEN SUTRA EVERY SANZO CARRIES.
OI, SANZO.
TELL ME WHY WE'RE WASTING OUR TIME AGAIN?
THE KID SAID A SANZO PRIEST WAS TAKEN HERE.
IF HE REALLY WAS KILLED BY THAT YOUKAI...
IT SEEMS THAT GYUMAOH'S FORCE IS GATHERING SUTRAS.
RIGHT.
WHICH IS WHY WE NEED TO FIND IT FIRST.
NN?

?!
WHAT THE-- NYAGH!
HEY!
M-MY BODY'S SINKIN'!
GOKU!
WHAT THE HELL'S--
!!

DAMMIT!
WHA?!
YOU'RE SHITTIN' ME!
WATCH IT, GOJYO!

!!
NNGH!

GREAT.
IS THIS A TRAP?

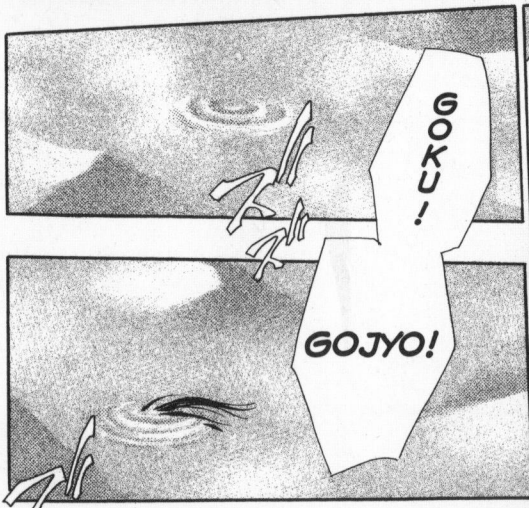
GOKU!
GOJYO!

I'D SAY THAT'S A REASON-ABLE GUESS.
HAH!

SNAG
JEEP ?!
ズ
ズ
ズ…

ギリ
ギリ
ギリ

NO, DON'T!
LET GO BEFORE YOU'RE PULLED IN WITH US!
ズ
ズ

ばい
!
ズ
ズ
ズ
ズ…
ア…

CHEEP!

CHEEP CHEEP!

CHEEEEEEP!

オオオオ

第29話

CHAPTER 29: A FATAL DOSE

THERE YOU ARE, LADY LIRIN.
I WAS LOOKING FOR YOU.
LADY GYOKUMEN WANTS TO SEE YOU.
YO, YAONE.
YES?

WAS ONII-CHAN'S MOM A NICE LADY?

HE LOVES HER A LOT, SO SHE'S GOTTA BE NICE.

MAYBE ONII-CHAN'S MOM'LL LOVE ME INSTEAD.
I KNOW MY MAMA HATES ME.

LIRIN, LISTEN.
BLOOD ISN'T EVERYTHING.
AND REMEMBER SOMETHING...
LADY LIRIN...
MAYBE SHE WON'T CARE IF I'M HER REAL KID OR NOT.
YOUR BROTHER AND I LOVE YOU VERY MUCH.
LIRIN LOVES YOU TOO.
I KNOW. NYA HA!

ふっ
……
WHERE THE HELL... AM I?

COME TO THINK OF IT, I CAN'T MOVE A THING.
DRUGS, MAYBE.
...AND MY ARMS WON'T MOVE. GREAT.
I GUESS THAT YOUKAI'S LOOKING FOR COMPANY.
ARE WE AWAKE ALREADY?
IT'S ALL RIGHT; THERE'S NO RUSH.
IF YOU'RE STUCK IN THAT BE,D YOU MIGHT AS WELL ENJOY IT.

I'M LIAN LI, MASTER OF THIS CASTLE.
AND HOW ARE WE FEELING, DEAR PRIEST SANZO?
LIKE... SHIT.
DAMN, EVEN MY MOUTH BARELY MOVES.
THAT'S TOO BAD.
YOUR FRIENDS? BEING ENTERTAINED ELSEWHERE.
WHERE... ARE THEY?
BUT FORGET ABOUT THEM.

I ADMIT I'M SURPRISED.
YOU'RE THE SECOND SANZO TO WANDER TO MY HOME.

...YOU ATE THE OTHER ONE?
WITH RELISH.
HE TASTED BETTER THAN HE LOOKED.

THE OTHER SANZO CHANTED A SUTRA AND ALMOST WET HIMSELF.
I THOUGHT ALL HIGH PRIESTS WERE STRAIGHT-LACED OLD MEN.
A PRETTY YOUNG THING LIKE YOU'S A TREAT.

YOU DON'T SEEM AFRAID. WHY?
N-NO REASON.

SO YOU'RE ALREADY... IMMORTAL.
WHY BOTHER EATING ME?
I THINK I LIKE YOU.
AFTER YOU CAME ALL THE WAY HERE? NOT EATING YOU WOULD BE RUDE.
T-TELL ME.
WHAT'S THE DRAW OF BEING AGELESS?
I SEE YOU'RE NOT AN EXPERT ON WOMEN.
WE WANT TO STAY BEAUTIFUL FOREVER, SANZO.
G-GREAT.

EXCUSE ME?
YOUR MAKEUP'S PRETTY... THICK.
BUT NOT THICK ENOUGH.
YOU'RE ABSOLUTELY VOMIT-WORTHY.
BUT YOU'RE NOT FOOLING ANYONE, FAGGOT.
TAKE THAT BACK, PRIEST.

YOU'RE STUCK IN THAT UGLY BODY FOR ETERNITY.

I'M NOT THE LOSER HERE.

YOU'RE IN NO POSITION TO THROW AROUND INSULTS.

I CAN KILL YOU WHENEVER I WANT!

JUST G-GET GOING.

OI! OI OI OI OI!

ガーン

LET US OUTTA HERE!

ガーン

ARE YA LISTENIN', UGLIES?! OI!
ガッシャ
I DON'T THINK ASKING IS ENOUGH TO GET US OUT.
ガッシャ
GIVE IT A REST, GOKU.

SHE'S WELCOME TO FRICKIN' TRY.
ALTHOUGH I DON'T ENVY SANZO DURING THAT.

BUT SANZO'S GONE!
THAT YOUKAI'S GONNA TRY TO EAT 'IM!

FIRST THINGS FIRST, GOKU.
WE NEED TO PLAN AN ESCAPE.
ガ
MMM...

YOU USED ALL YOUR ENERGY THRASHING AT THE BARS.
HM. BEFORE SANZO CAN BE EATEN...
I TOLD YOU TO QUIT IT.
I'M SO HUUUNGRY.
...OUR GOKU JUST MAY STARVE.

TWITCH
.....?

CLAMP
SOME SORTA "FWAPPY FWAPPY" SOUND LIKE--

WHAT'S THAT SOUND?
GREAT. YOU'RE HEARING THINGS NOW?
AM NOT! IT'S LIKE... PAPER MOVIN'.

COME NOW. THIS IS THE DESERT.
A SCORPION OR TWO ISN'T...
NYAAAA!
GOKU?
A SCORPION! GET IT OFF GET IT OFF!

R-RIGHT. ONE OR TWO I CAN SEE.
BUT WHAT'S A MILLION SUPPOSED TO MEAN?

I DON'T THINK IT'S POSSIBLE, MASTER.
THANK YOU FOR THE THOUGHT...
...BUT I'M NOT WORTHY TO BE A SANZO PRIEST.
LISTEN TO ME, KOURYUU.
THERE WERE NEVER ANY CRITERIA FOR BECOMING A SANZO.
IT'S BEEN THIRTEEN YEARS, BUT I THINK I SEE NOW.
A SANZO NEEDS A STRONG BODY...
...BUT, MORE IMPORTANTLY, HE NEEDS A STRONG

IT'S TIME FOR YOU TO BE STRONG...
...PRIEST GENJYO SANZO.
AND THOSE WORDS OF HIS WERE THE LAST HE EVER SAID.
IT WAS THE LAST SMILE HE EVER MADE.
MY PRIESTHOOD WAS MY MASTER'S FINAL WISH!

KOUMYOU SANZO.
MY TEACHER. MY FATHER.
HE WAS THE ONLY SANZO PRIEST I EVER ACKNOWLEDGED.
THE FACT THAT I NOW CARRY MY MASTER'S NAME...
...SERVES TO REMIND ME OF MY OWN FALLIBILITY.
HUNH.
YOU'RE A COCKY LITTLE BASTARD, AREN'T YOU?
NNGH.
HAH.
SPLAT

...MAYBE YOU'RE RIGHT.
YOU'RE ALL THE SAME IN THE END.
THERE'S NO POWER IN STUPID HUMANS READING SUTRAS!
WHAT'S SO GREAT ABOUT A SANZO PRIEST?!
YOU'RE NOTHING BUT FOOD TO ME!
DINNER'S ALL YOU ARE--

HGCK!
WH-
WHAT?
BUT YOU SHOULDN'T BE ABLE TO MOVE!

YOU'RE RIGHT, BY THE WAY. A SANZO'S NOTHING BUT A HUMAN.
BUT HUMANS ARE GOOD AT KILLING.
YOUR *BITCH SLAPS* WERE ENOUGH TO WEAR THE DRUGS DOWN.

GIVE ME A BREAK.
YOU ACTUALLY BELIEVE THAT STUPID RUMOR?
HA HA HA!
FORGETTING SOMETHING?
I'M *IMMORTAL*, SANZO. YOU CAN'T KILL ME!
ANYONE WHO THINKS EATING A HUMAN WILL MAKE YOU AGELESS IS A MORON.
I'M GUESSING YOU'VE NEVER HAD PROOF OF YOUR IMMORTALITY.
.....!!

CARE TO TEST THAT THEORY OUT?

SMITH&WESSON
カチ
カチ!!
OW!
!
N-NO!

IF I HIT YOUR HEAD OR HEART...
...I BET IT'D HURT LIKE HELL.
NO!
PLEASE, DON'T!
LOOK AT THAT.
I GUESS IMMORTALS CAN FEEL PAIN LIKE THE REST OF US.
AAAAAAGH!

THIS IS STUPID.
YAAAAAH!
AAAH!
THIS IS REALLY STUPID.
GYAAAAAH!

WHAT'RE YOU DOIN', SANZO?!
huff

.....!

SHIT, MAN! TORTURE?
THIS ISN'T LIKE YOU!
NOT LIKE ME...?

WHAT'S THAT SUPPOSED TO...
THEN WHAT IS LIKE ME?

GOKU?

OW!

HIT ME WITH TH' FAN AND CALL ME STUPID MONKEY.
OKAY?
THAT'S WHAT SANZO'S LIKE.
.....
THAT HURT!
WHAT THE HELL ARE YOU DOING?!
HIT ME.

YOU.
ANSWER ME SOME-THING.
I SUPPOSE IT COULDN'T STAND UP TO GOKU.
HOW VERY SUDDEN.
THAT CRUELTY IN SANZO JUST VANISHED COMPLETELY.
WHERE ARE YOU HIDING THE SUTRAS?
I WANT MINE AND I WANT THE OTHER SANZO'S.
SO GET TALKING.
TH-THE SUTRAS?

THERE?
THE OLD ONE'S S-SOMEWHERE AROUND THE CASTLE.
YOURS IS IN THE CHEST.
THE ONE RIGHT BEHIND YOU.
はっ
SANZO, WATCH IT!

GAHAH!

SANZO!
ARE YOU OKAY?!
HAKKAI, FIX HIM!
CALM DOWN, GOK--
?!
WHAT?

HEH HEH. DO YOU L-LIKE MY SCORPION CLAWS?
THE POISON IN THEM'S FATAL.
!
YOU... YOU STUPID CREEP!

DAMN. HOT ENOUGH FOR YA?

MM.

BUT THAT'S STRANGE.

ACCORDING TO THE REPORT, THE CASTLE SHOULD BE HERE.

?

SOMETHING WRONG, DOKUGAKU?
UH, NO.
THERE'S JUST SOME WHITE THING BURIED OVER THERE.
?!
HEY, LOOK AT THAT!
ISN'T THAT THE, UH...

IT SURE LOOKS LIKE SANZO'S JEEP.
WHAT'S IT DOING HERE?
?
CHEEEP
CHEEEP
CHEEP
I DON'T BELIEVE THIS.
SANZO AND THE OTHERS ARE HERE!

オリジナルビデオアニメ よこくへん
OVA予告編
HELLO, SANZO AND COMPANY!
THE NEXT "ACCIDENT" IS ABOUT TO BEGIN.
I DO HOPE EVERYONE'S READY.

PASSING THROUGH THE VILLAGE...
永安酒家
...I TAKE IT YOU MADE SOME NEW FRIENDS?
AND YOU'RE WELCOME OVER HERE, SWEETHEART. ♡
Sha Gojyo (Voice Actor: Kouichi Yamadera)
YOUR JEEP IS AMAZING! YOU'RE ALL VERY WELCOME HERE. ♡
Son Goku (Voice Actor: Kosuke Okano)
THERE'S A FESTIVAL TODAY. COME CELEBRATE WITH US!
THESE'RE FIREWORKS?

HIS NAME IS JEEP. DO YOU LIKE HIM?
Cho Hakkai (Voice Actor: Akira Ishida)
EASY ON MY CREDIT CARD, DIMWITS.
Genjyo Sanzo (Voice Actor: Wataru Takagi)
YOU BOYS'RE STRONG!
EAT AS MUCH AS YOU WANT.
AH, FICKLE LIFE.
ACCIDENTS ARE SUCH A SHAME.

SOUNDS LIKE SOME KINDA FIRECRACK--
ボン!!
HYA HA HA!
HA HA!

!!!
……
HYA HA HA HA HA!
THAT'S NOT FRICKIN' F-FUNNY.

BUT PLEASE.
I CAN'T JUST IGNORE THIS!
ENSUI CONSIDERS HIMSELF AN EXPLOSION ARTIST.
YAONE...
HE'S REALLY MORE OF A MAD SCIENTIST THAN ANYTHING.
CALL ME MOMMY.
MM.
COME, KOUGAIJI DEAR. DON'T BE SHY.

GET AWAY FROM HIM, JEEP!
THE MOMENT A SOUL SHATTERS IS TRULY ART!
ISN'T IT BEAUTI-FUL?
DON'T WORRY-- I'LL LET HIM GO.
YOU'RE MY FRIENDS.
BROTHERS, EVEN.
FELLOW YOUKAI.
Y-YOU LIAR!

WHAT'S THAT NOISE?
IT CAN'T BE...!
THE COUNT-DOWN BEGINS.
THAT'S RIGHT, BOYS.
YOUR PET IS NOW CARRYING A TIME BOMB.
I CAN'T GET IT OUT.
IT'S EATEN INTO JEEP'S NERVES!

05:55
FIVE AND THREE-QUARTERS, REALLY.
YOU HAVE SIX HOURS.
WELL...
LEAVE US ALONE, YA STUPID PSYCHO!
WHAT'D WE EVER DO TO YOU?!
.....
PRE-PARE TO DIE.
THESE ARE ONLY ACCIDENTS.
AND ACCIDENTS ARE NOBODY'S FAULT.

オリジナルビデオ アニメ アンド ディー ブイ ディー さいゆうき

OVA&DVD最遊記

OVA & DVD SAIYUKI

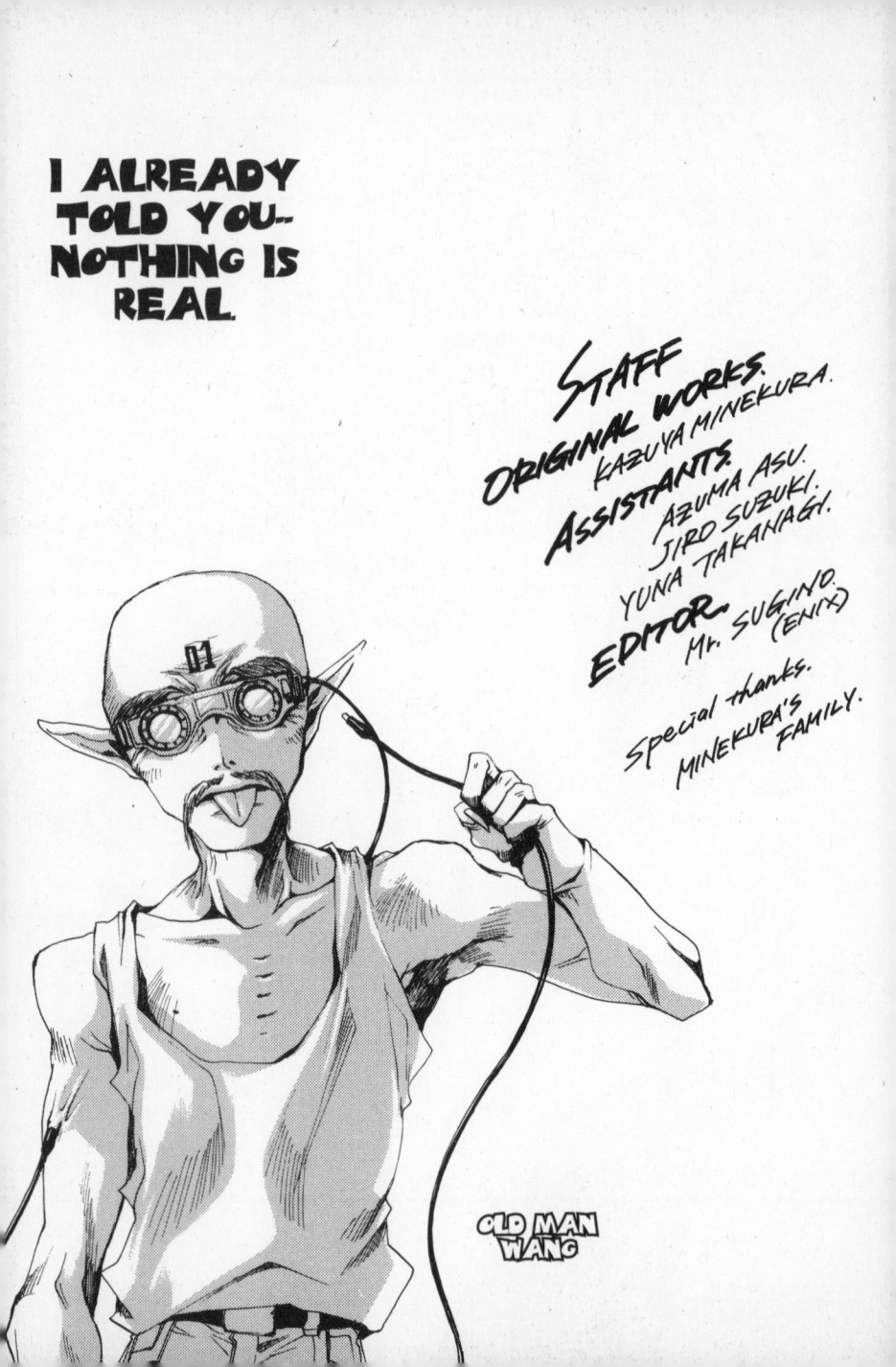
I ALREADY TOLD YOU-- NOTHING IS REAL.
STAFF
ORIGINAL WORKS.
KAZUYA MINEKURA.
ASSISTANTS.
AZUMA ASU.
JIRO SUZUKI.
YUNA TAKANAGI.
EDITOR.
Mr. SUGINO. (ENIX)
Special thanks.
MINEKURA'S FAMILY.
OLD MAN WANG

GETTING WET IS STUPID IN THIS COLD.
to the skin.
KAZUYA MINEKURA 1999.

Get soaked

SOUND EFFECT CHART

THE FOLLOWING IS A LIST OF THE SOUND EFFECTS USED IN SAIYUKI. EACH SOUND IS LABELED BY PAGE AND PANEL NUMBER, SEPARATED BY A PERIOD. THE FIRST DESCRIPTION (IN BOLD) IS THE PHONETIC READING OF THE JAPANESE, AND IS FOLLOWED BY THE EQUIVALENT ENGLISH SOUND OR A DESCRIPTION.

GIRI!

THIS USEFUL SOUND EFFECT HAS A COUPLE OF FUNCTIONS: IT CAN BE EITHER THE SOUND OF GRINDING TEETH OR TWO COMBATANTS STRUGGLING AGAINST EACH OTHER.

26.5 UGAA: GRR
27.4 SU: (MOVING SILENTLY)
30.7 ZAWA ZAWA: CHATTER
32.2 GATAN: CLATTER
33.2 KII: CREAK
33.4 BASA: FLUTTER
37.4 GATA: CLATTER
37.5 GACHA: LATCH
38.4 KII: CREAK
38.5 PATAN: SHUT
43.3 ZAH: DODGE
43.4 PASHI: GRAB
44.1 DOGOH: SLAM
44.2 GAKU: DROOP
44.3 KERA, GOHO: COUGH
9.2 GOHOH: GLUB
13.4 GATA: CLATTER
13.7 ZAA: (FALLING RAIN)
15.2 ZAA: (FALLING RAIN)
15.3 GUH: NUDGE
16.3 ZAA (FALLING RAIN)
18.2 ZUKI: THROB
18.3 PUHAA: PUFF
21.1 DORO: MUDDY
21.3 PAN!: FWAP!
22.2 BOSO BOSO: WHISPER
22.5 BIKU: SURPRISE
22.6 ZAH: STEP

DOKUN!

IN MOST MANGA, A PLEASANT LITTLE "DOKI DOKI" IS THE PREFERRED SOUND FOR HEARTBEATS, BUT IN SAIYUKI, THEY NEEDED TO KICK IT UP A NOTCH. "DOKUN" IS THE SOUND OF A PARTICULARLY STRONG HEARTBEAT, USUALLY RESERVED FOR MOMENTS OF EXTREME SHOCK OR DEMONIC TRANSFORMATION.

53.4 ZAH: GRAB
53.5 BAH: MOVE
53.5 KICHU: SCREACH

NIKO! (OR JUST NI)

IT TAKES 26 MUSCLES TO SMILE, OR JUST TWO KATAKANA! "NIKO," REPEATED AS MUCH AS YOU WANT FOR EMPHASIS, GIVES THE READER AN INDICATION OF JUST HOW BIG A SMILE IS.

56.1 ZAKU...: WHOOSH
56.2 KOPOPO: GLUB GLUB
56.5 ZU: SLURP
56.6 ZUZUZU: SLURP SLURP SLURP
59.3 GOTSUN GOTSUN: NOD NOD
60.1 UHAA: WOO-HOO!
60.2 GYAA GYAA: RANT RANT
60.3 GUGIGI: SQUEEZE (HEADLOCK)
64.1 GATA: CLATTER
65.2 ZURU...: SLIDE
65.6 GOSO: RUSTLE
66.1 JARA...: CRACK
66.5 GOH: WHOOSH
67.1 DOGOH!: SLAM
67.2 DOSA: THUD
67.3 JARI: SCRAPE
68.2 DOKUN: THADUMP
70.1 GIRI: SCUFF
70.3 KOTOH: CLULNK
74.4 JII: STARE

44.4 GAH: GRAB
45.1 BAKU: PUNCH
45.2 ZAZAH: WHOOSH
45.3 GUH: WIPE
46.5 GAUN: BANG
46.6 HIKU: TWITCH
47.1 GACHA: LATCH
47.3 BAH: MOVE
47.4 HYU: WHOOSH
47.5 PASHI: KICK
47.6 KASHA: CLUNK
48.1 GO: LIFT...
48.2 ZUSHA: SLAM
48.3 GIRI: GRIT
49.3 DAH: DASH
49.5 TAAN: THUD
50.3 ZAH: RUSH
50.4 GAH: KICK
50.6 BAH: SHOVE
51.1 JAH...: THUD
51.4 KURU: TURN
51.4 WAKU WAKU: GIDDY
52.1 GOPAA: WHACK
52-53 DOSA: THUD
53.3 DAH: DASH

L SHIN! h.

THE SOUND OF SILENCE. THE PERFECT "SOUND" EFFECT TO PUNCTUATE THOSE UNCOMFORTABLE MOMENTS WHERE THE LACK OF ANY ACTUAL SOUNDS JUST ISN'T SUFFICIENT. FOR EMPHASIS, YOU'LL USUALLY SEE A LONG LINE IN BETWEEN THE "SHI" AND THE "N," INDICATING PROLONGED SILENCE.

112.1 TOH: GLOMP
113.2 KATAH: CLUNK
115.1 GABAH: GLOMP
115.3 BAN: SLAM
116.2 BAH: RUSH

HAH!

はっ

THIS IS ONE OF THE MOST COMMON SOUNDS YOU'LL SEE IN MANGA. IT'S USED TO INDICATE SURPRISE AND IS USUALLY EQUIVALENT TO "GASP!" "H" ISN'T NECESSARILY VOCALIZED, THOUGH.

121.2: KAH: FLASH
122.1-4 DODODODO: RUUUUMBLE
122.4 CHAKI: CLICK
123.1 BURORORO: VROOM
123.3 DODODO: RUUUMBLE
124.1 DODO: RUUUMBLE
124.2 DODODO: RUUUMBLE
126.2 BASA: RUSTLE
127.3 SHIIIN: SILENCE
131.5 ZAAH: WHOOSH
133.2 OOOH: HOWLING WIND
133.3 KA KA KA: CLICK
138.5 PETAPETA: WAVE WAVE
139.2 ZUN ZUN: SNIFF SNIFF
139.5 PAAA: YAAAY
141.2 OOO: HOLWING WIND
142.4 ZAAA: HOWLING WIND
143.1 ZUBU: SINK
143.2 GAKUN: DROOP
143.3 ZUZUZU: SINK SINK SINK
143.4 GAKUN: DROOP

76.4 PIKU: PERK
77.2-3 ZAAH: WHOOSH
79.1 GUH: GRAB
79.3 BUSHU: SCOOP OUT
79.4 PASHI: SPIT
79.5 BISHA: SPLAT
81.2 SOH: SHIVER
81.3 GUH: GRAB
81.4 ZAZA: RUN RUN
82.1 BAH: GLOMP
82.2 DOSA: THUD
82.3 KYOTO: LOOK
86.2 GATAKU: SHIVER
86.3 DAH: DASH
86.4 GOH: WHOOSH
87.2 PAAN: BANG
90-91 OOOH: HOWLING WIND
91.3 SHARI: SCUFF
92.2 OOO: HOWLING WIND
93.4 BAH: SIT

ZAA!

YOU'LL SEE THIS ONE A LOT IN *SAIYUKI*. "ZAA" INDICATES A DRAMATIC APPEARANCE. IF YOU WANT TO MAKE A LASTING IMPRESSION, ALWAYS COME IN WITH A COOL POSE AND A BIG "ZAA!"

96.2 OOOH: HOWLING WIND
98.2 GOUN: BOOM
101.2 GAH: GRAB
108.3 TAH: TMP
111.4 GYAA GYAA: RANT RANT

155.5 GISHI: CREAK
158.2 PIKU: TWITCH
158.4 PAAN: SLAP
159.4 GAN GAN: CLANG CLANG
160.1 GASHA GASHA: CLANG CLANG
160.5 ZU: SLIP
161.1 ZURUZURU: SLIP
162.2 BOTO: PLOP
163.2 ZAKU: SKITTER
166.3 BAKII: PUNK/WHACK
167.1 GUI: TUG
167.5 HYU: WHOOSH
168.1 BAKI: PUNCH/WHACK
168.2 DOSA: THUD
169.2 ZAH: STEP
171.4 GAUN: BANG
173.1 GAUN: BANG
173.2 GAUN: BANG
173.3 GAUN: BANG
174.1 BAN: SLAM
174.3 GUI: GRAB
175.4 GAN: KICK
177.5 ZEH ZEH: PANT PANT
178.4 HA: GASP
178.5 SHAKII: GLEAM
179.1 BUSHU: THUNK
182.1 OOOH: HOWLING WIND
183.1 ZAH: STEP
184.4 OOOH: HOWLING WIND
188.3 WAAA: LOUD CROWD
189.1 BURORORO: VROOM
190.1 GOH: WHOOSH
190.2 DOOON: BOOOM
190.3 GOOOO: HOWLING WIND
191.2 DAH: DASH
193.2 BAH: RUSH
194.1 PACHIN: SNAP
143.4 GAKUN: DROOP
144.1 ZUZUZU: SINK SINK SINK
144.2 GAH: GRAB
145.1 ZUZUZU: SINK SINK SINK
145.3 ZUBA: SINK
145.4 ZUZUZU: SINK SINK SINK
146.2 ZUZUZU: SINK SINK SINK
146.3 GIRI GIRI: GRIT
146.4 ZUZU: SINK SINK
147.1 BAH: SHOVE

#9 ZAWA!

NO ONE REALLY CARES WHAT ALL THOSE EXTRAS IN THE BACKGROUND ARE SAYING, RIGHT? THAT'S WHY MANGA-KA USE THIS HANDY SOUND EFFECT TO INDICATE BACKGROUND CHATTER. YOU'LL SEE IT HOVERING OVER CROWDED CITY STREETS OR CLASSROOMS THROUGHOUT MANGA. IT CAN ALSO BE USED TO INDICATE THE SOUND OF WIND BLOWING THROUGH THE LEAVES OF A TREE. AIN'T THAT SWEET?

147.2 ZUZU: SINK SINK
147.3 ZU...: SINK...
147.4 ZAA: RUSTLE
148.2 OOO: HOWLING WIND
150.2 HOH: GASP
153.3 FU...: SIGH
154.1 PIKU: TWITCH
154.3 PATA: THUD
154.6 KAH: CLACK

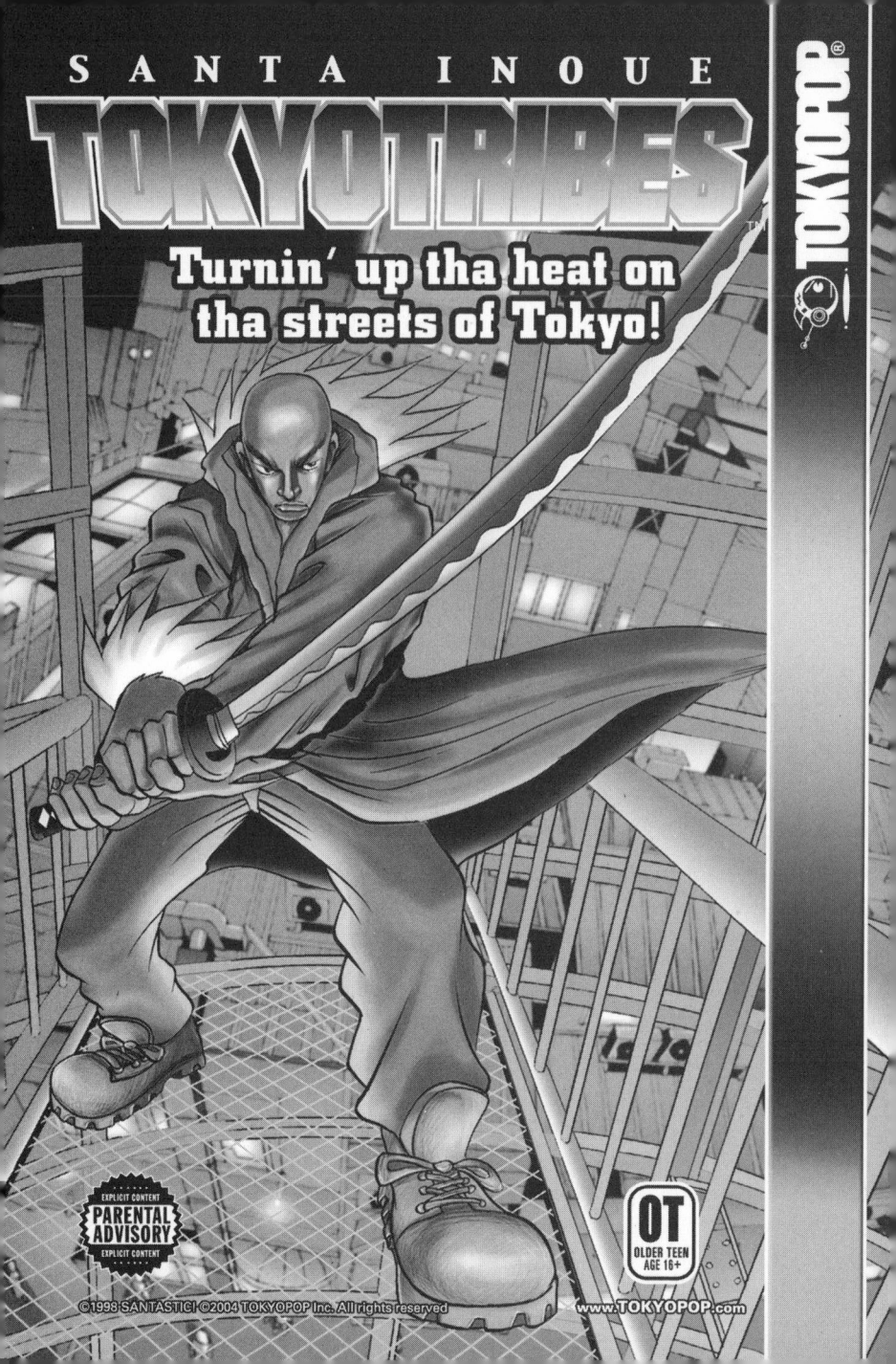
SANTA INOUE
TOKYOTRIBES™
Turnin' up tha heat on tha streets of Tokyo!
TOKYOPOP®
EXPLICIT CONTENT
PARENTAL ADVISORY
EXPLICIT CONTENT
OT
OLDER TEEN
AGE 16+
©1998 SANTASTIC! ©2004 TOKYOPOP Inc. All rights reserved
www.TOKYOPOP.com

TOKYOPOP®

BASED ON THE HIT VIDEO GAME SERIES!

Suikoden II

幻想水滸伝

A legendary hero.
A war with no future.
An epic for today.

T
TEEN
AGE 13+

www.TOKYOPOP.com

©2002 Aki Shimizu. ©1995, 2004 Konami Computer Entertainment. ©2004 TOKYOPOP Inc.

ShutterBox

TOKYOPOP®

LIKE A PHOTOGRAPH...
LOVE DEVELOPS IN DARKNESS

NEW GOTHIC SHOJO MANGA

AVAILABLE NOW AT YOUR FAVORITE BOOK AND COMIC STORES.

www.TOKYOPOP.com

ShutterBox © 2003 Rosearik Rikki Simons and Tavisha Wolfgang Simons Copyright © 2003 TOKYOPOP Inc. All rights reserved

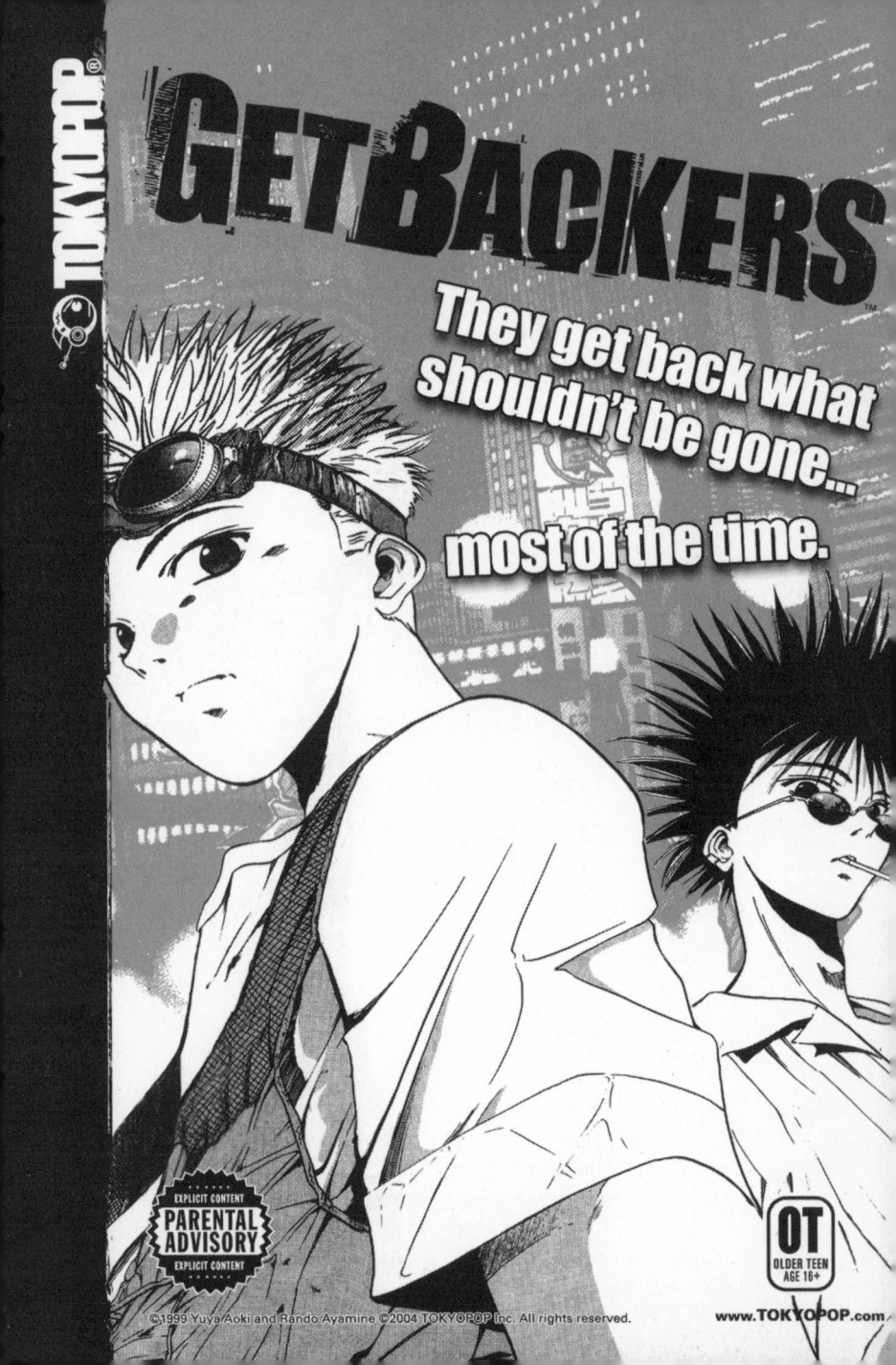
TOKYOPOP®
GETBACKERS™
They get back what shouldn't be gone...
most of the time.
EXPLICIT CONTENT
PARENTAL ADVISORY
EXPLICIT CONTENT
OT
OLDER TEEN
AGE 16+
©1999 Yuya Aoki and Rando Ayamine ©2004 TOKYOPOP Inc. All rights reserved.
www.TOKYOPOP.com

ALSO AVAILABLE FROM TOKYOPOP®

PET SHOP OF HORRORS
PITA-TEN
PLANET LADDER
PLANETES
PRIEST
PRINCESS AI
PSYCHIC ACADEMY
QUEEN'S KNIGHT, THE
RAGNAROK
RAVE MASTER
REALITY CHECK
REBIRTH
REBOUND
REMOTE
RISING STARS OF MANGA
SABER MARIONETTE J
SAILOR MOON
SAINT TAIL
SAIYUKI
SAMURAI DEEPER KYO
SAMURAI GIRL REAL BOUT HIGH SCHOOL
SCRYED
SEIKAI TRILOGY, THE
SGT. FROG
SHAOLIN SISTERS
SHIRAHIME-SYO: SNOW GODDESS TALES
SHUTTERBOX
SKULL MAN, THE
SNOW DROP
SORCERER HUNTERS
STONE
SUIKODEN III
SUKI
THREADS OF TIME
TOKYO BABYLON
TOKYO MEW MEW
TOKYO TRIBES
TRAMPS LIKE US
UNDER THE GLASS MOON
VAMPIRE GAME
VISION OF ESCAFLOWNE, THE
WARRIORS OF TAO
WILD ACT
WISH
WORLD OF HARTZ
X-DAY
ZODIAC P.I.

NOVELS

CLAMP SCHOOL PARANORMAL INVESTIGATORS
KARMA CLUB
SAILOR MOON
SLAYERS

ART BOOKS

ART OF CARDCAPTOR SAKURA
ART OF MAGIC KNIGHT RAYEARTH, THE
PEACH: MIWA UEDA ILLUSTRATIONS

ANIME GUIDES

COWBOY BEBOP
GUNDAM TECHNICAL MANUALS
SAILOR MOON SCOUT GUIDES

TOKYOPOP KIDS

STRAY SHEEP

CINE-MANGA™

ALADDIN
CARDCAPTORS
DUEL MASTERS
FAIRLY ODDPARENTS, THE
FAMILY GUY
FINDING NEMO
G.I. JOE SPY TROOPS
GREATEST STARS OF THE NBA
JACKIE CHAN ADVENTURES
JIMMY NEUTRON: BOY GENIUS, THE ADVENTURES OF
KIM POSSIBLE
LILO & STITCH: THE SERIES
LIZZIE MCGUIRE
LIZZIE MCGUIRE MOVIE, THE
MALCOLM IN THE MIDDLE
POWER RANGERS: DINO THUNDER
POWER RANGERS: NINJA STORM
PRINCESS DIARIES 2
RAVE MASTER
SHREK 2
SIMPLE LIFE, THE
SPONGEBOB SQUAREPANTS
SPY KIDS 2
SPY KIDS 3-D: GAME OVER
THAT'S SO RAVEN
TOTALLY SPIES
TRANSFORMERS: ARMADA
TRANSFORMERS: ENERGON
VAN HELSING

You want it? We got it!
A full range of TOKYOPOP products are available now at:
www.TOKYOPOP.com/shop

05.26.04T

ALSO AVAILABLE FROM TOKYOPOP®

MANGA

.HACK//LEGEND OF THE TWILIGHT
@LARGE
ABENOBASHI: MAGICAL SHOPPING ARCADE
A.I. LOVE YOU
AI YORI AOSHI
ANGELIC LAYER
ARM OF KANNON
BABY BIRTH
BATTLE ROYALE
BATTLE VIXENS
BRAIN POWERED
BRIGADOON
B'TX
CANDIDATE FOR GODDESS, THE
CARDCAPTOR SAKURA
CARDCAPTOR SAKURA - MASTER OF THE CLOW
CHOBITS
CHRONICLES OF THE CURSED SWORD
CLAMP SCHOOL DETECTIVES
CLOVER
COMIC PARTY
CONFIDENTIAL CONFESSIONS
CORRECTOR YUI
COWBOY BEBOP
COWBOY BEBOP: SHOOTING STAR
CRAZY LOVE STORY
CRESCENT MOON
CROSS
CULDCEPT
CYBORG 009
D•N•ANGEL
DEMON DIARY
DEMON ORORON, THE
DEUS VITAE
DIABOLO
DIGIMON
DIGIMON TAMERS
DIGIMON ZERO TWO
DOLL
DRAGON HUNTER
DRAGON KNIGHTS
DRAGON VOICE
DREAM SAGA
DUKLYON: CLAMP SCHOOL DEFENDERS
EERIE QUEERIE!
ERICA SAKURAZAWA: COLLECTED WORKS
ET CETERA
ETERNITY
EVIL'S RETURN
FAERIES' LANDING
FAKE
FLCL
FLOWER OF THE DEEP SLEEP
FORBIDDEN DANCE
FRUITS BASKET
G GUNDAM
GATEKEEPERS
GETBACKERS
GIRL GOT GAME
GIRLS EDUCATIONAL CHARTER
GRAVITATION
GTO
GUNDAM BLUE DESTINY
GUNDAM SEED ASTRAY
GUNDAM WING
GUNDAM WING: BATTLEFIELD OF PACIFISTS
GUNDAM WING: ENDLESS WALTZ
GUNDAM WING: THE LAST OUTPOST (G-UNIT)
GUYS' GUIDE TO GIRLS
HANDS OFF!
HAPPY MANIA
HARLEM BEAT
HYPER RUNE
I.N.V.U.
IMMORTAL RAIN
INITIAL D
INSTANT TEEN: JUST ADD NUTS
ISLAND
JING: KING OF BANDITS
JING: KING OF BANDITS - TWILIGHT TALES
JULINE
KARE KANO
KILL ME, KISS ME
KINDAICHI CASE FILES, THE
KING OF HELL
KODOCHA: SANA'S STAGE
LAMENT OF THE LAMB
LEGAL DRUG
LEGEND OF CHUN HYANG, THE
LES BIJOUX
LOVE HINA
LUPIN III
LUPIN III: WORLD'S MOST WANTED
MAGIC KNIGHT RAYEARTH I
MAGIC KNIGHT RAYEARTH II
MAHOROMATIC: AUTOMATIC MAIDEN
MAN OF MANY FACES
MARMALADE BOY
MARS
MARS: HORSE WITH NO NAME
MINK
MIRACLE GIRLS
MIYUKI-CHAN IN WONDERLAND
MODEL
MOURYOU KIDEN
MY LOVE
NECK AND NECK
ONE
ONE I LOVE, THE
PARADISE KISS
PARASYTE
PASSION FRUIT
PEACH GIRL
PEACH GIRL: CHANGE OF HEART

05.26.04T

FROM CLAMP, CREATORS OF CHOBITS.

TOKYO BABYLON™

Welcome to Tokyo.
The city never sleeps.
May its spirits rest in peace.

T
TEEN
AGE 13+

©1991 CLAMP. ©2004 TOKYOPOP Inc. All Rights Reserved.

www.TOKYOPOP.com

TOKYOPOP®